VH1 Music First BEHIND THE MUSIC™

CASUALTIES of ROCK

QUINTON
SKINNER

POCKET BOOKS
New York • London • Toronto • Sydney • Singapore

An *Original* Publication of VH1 Books/ Pocket Books

Music First

POCKET BOOKS, a division of Simon & Schuster Inc. 1230 Avenue of the Americas, New York, NY 10020

ISBN: 0-671-03963-6

First VH1 Books/Pocket Books trade paperback printing October 2001

10 9 8 7 6 5 4 3 2 1

POCKET and colophon are registered trademarks of Simon & Schuster Inc.

Cover and interior design by Nicholas Caruso, Nathan Savage, and Andrea Sepic/Red Herring Design

Printed in the U.S.A.

Cover photos: Front (top to bottom) London Features; CORBIS; © Michael DoGo/Michael Ochs Archives; Photofest; Photofest Back: Top(left to right) STARFILE PHOTO; STARFILE PHOTO; CORBIS; Photofest; Side(top to bottom) CORBIS; Photofest; CORBIS

For Gabriel

Thanks to Jacob Hoye and Wendy Walker
for their encouragement and support—and
for keeping it fun.

Also thanks to:

Paul Gallagher, Fred Graver, Jonathan Hyams
@ Michael Ochs, Dean Lubensky,
Lisa Masuda, JoAnna Myers, George Moll,
Donna O'Neill, Red Herring Design,
Janet Rollé, Jeri Rose, Gay Rosenthal,
Ann Sarnoff, Robin Silverman, Liate Stehlik,
John Sykes, Kara Welsh, and
Nancy Abbott Young

Contents

6   Introduction
10   G. G. Allin
11   The Allman Brothers Band
13   Badfinger
15   The Band
17   Syd Barrett
21   Stiv Bators
22   The Beach Boys
25   Chris Bell
26   Marc Bolan
28   Tommy Bolin
29   John Bonham
31   Sonny Bono
33   D. Boon
34   The Buckleys
37   Cliff Burton
38   Karen Carpenter
40   Harry Chapin
42   Gene Clark
44   Steve Clark
45   Kurt Cobain
48   Eddie Cochran
50   Sam Cooke
52   Jim Croce
53   Ian Curtis
55   The Day the Music Died: Buddy Holly, Ritchie Valens, The Big Bopper
59   Pete De Freitas
60   Sandy Denny
61   John Denver
63   Nicholas "Razzle" Dingley
64   Nick Drake
66   Eazy-E
68   Richey Edwards
69   Brian Epstein
71   Roky Erickson
73   Bobby Fuller
74   Marvin Gaye Jr.
77   Lowell George
78   Andy Gibb
80   The Grateful Dead
84   Peter Green
86   The Heartbreakers
87   Jimi Hendrix
90   Shannon Hoon

91   Michael Hutchence
93   Brian Jones
96   Janis Joplin
99   Terry Kath
100   Paul Kossoff
101   Ronnie Lane
102   John Lennon
105   Phil Lynott
107   Lynyrd Skynyrd
109   The Mamas and the Papas
111   Bob Marley
114   Curtis Mayfield
116   Paul McCartney
118   Freddie Mercury
120   Keith Moon
122   Jim Morrison
125   Rick Nelson
127   Nico
128   Harry Nilsson
129   Notorious B.I.G.
130   Phil Ochs
132   Roy Orbison
134   Gram Parsons
136   Rob Pilatus
138   Jeff Porcaro
139   Elvis Presley
143   The Pretenders
145   Joey Ramone
147   Otis Redding
149   Keith Relf
150   Randy Rhoads
151   Mark Sandman
152   Bon Scott
154   Tupac Shakur
157   Del Shannon
159   Hillel Slovak
160   Bob Stinson
161   Peter Tosh
164   Stevie Ray Vaughan
166   Sid Vicious
169   Gene Vincent
171   Wendy O. Williams
172   Jackie Wilson
173   Frank Zappa
176   Bibliography

Introduction

Certain occupations come laden with considerable occupational risk. Mining coal means facing the constant dangers of shafts collapsing, poisonous gas, and the long-term specter of black-lung disease. Driving a cab in a big city means living with the possibility of gunpoint robbery and high-speed crashes. And the high-rise window washer eyes his scaffolding every day and hopes this won't be the morning when the ropes finally break. Across the world, men and women get up and go to jobs that put their lives in jeopardy. They assess risks with open eyes and decide to soldier on another day.

And then there's the rock star.

I should have such problems, you might say. Money, fame, freedom. Fleets of cars, mansions, endless sexual opportunity, drugs, and thousands of faces looking up at you, singing along with the songs you wrote, feeding your ego until it inflates to the size of a zeppelin.

Could you handle it? Or would you become a casualty?

King Tutankhamen himself could not have imagined the luxury and indulgence available to the postwar, late-twentieth-century rock 'n' roll star. Money, mind-altering substances of every possible variety, the ability (and obligation) to travel the world, easy sex, and—perhaps most dangerous—the identity-warping prism of fame. Sometimes stardom grips a young person's life in its jaws and shakes him like an angry dog. And sometimes the man or woman doesn't survive the experience.

Turns out being a rock 'n' roll star is a damned dangerous line of work.

Time and again an artist's ego has proven too fragile to handle the white-knuckle rush of fame. It starts innocently, with a boy of ten standing in front of a mirror, practicing his rock-star moves with an old tennis racquet. In the kitchen there's a little girl singing, imagining herself on a stage and knowing her voice is her ticket *out* of wherever and whoever she doesn't want to be.

The boy grows into a talented adolescent, forms a band, hones his craft, and eventually lands a recording contract. Success—it's what he lives for. It's what drives him, the tantalizing vision that ushers him into his dreams every night. He's going to be heard, he's going to show the world a thing or two. He's going to be *somebody*, and he's going to make the whole world *listen*.

And then it all happens at once. He breaks it big with a single, then releases a hit album. He films videos and tours the world. His face peers out from the covers of *Rolling Stone* and *Time*.

That little boy is a man now, and he's made it. He's a rock star. It's all he ever lived for, and now that it's happened . . . what's next?

Maybe he starts taking drugs because he can't sleep—he's too hyper after performing and strung out from constant travel. He doesn't know where all the money is going, or even how much money he has; his manager says not to worry, but he does, all the time. He looks around at all the people in his employ—the

handlers, the promoters, the accountants, the attorneys—they're all taking a cut of his money, and he has no idea who he can trust. The pressure builds, and soon he feels estranged from his family and his band. He knows the girls throwing themselves at him are interested only in his image; they don't know anything about *him*.

And who is he, anyway? He sits in a hotel room alone watching himself on TV, barely recognizing the man on the screen as himself. He starts to drink too much, his record company is demanding another album, and he can't tell them he's out of songs and that he needs some time off. He surrounds himself with bodyguards after getting a couple of letters from fanatics threatening his life. He's losing touch. He knows something is wrong, that his life is out of control. He's going to fix things, he's going to get better. He's just not sure when. Or how.

If he's not careful, he's going to become a rock 'n' roll casualty.

Elvis. Lennon. Hendrix. Morrison. Joplin. Cobain. Moon. Start listing the rockers who didn't make it and the names just keep on coming.

The history of rock 'n' roll is riddled with mistakes, miscues, and genuine tragedy. For every rocker who has reached middle age and, inevitably, reunited with his old band for a cash-raking stroll across the stage, there is another who didn't survive. More often than not, rock stars succumb to their own vices and recklessness. But anyone tempted to dismiss their deaths as just desserts for spoiled children

should ask themselves: *Would I have done any better? Would I have made it through?*

Casualties of Rock is a memorial to those rockers who didn't survive, as well as a handful whose minds were shattered by rock 'n' roll fame. We remember their stories in light of what they accomplished when they shone their brightest. And we recount their downfalls because it is an essential aspect of their legacy. Their stories should be told with appropriate fascination, respect, and humor—because we're still dealing with rock 'n' roll. Rock's place isn't in a museum, with stone-faced curators and hushed devotees filing past the music's relics and monuments. The essence of rock 'n' roll is excitement, irreverence, and the immediacy of the moment. Rock 'n' roll's essence is forgetting responsibilities and cares. It's based on moments such as meeting someone's eyes across a crowded room and knowing your life has changed forever.

The artists in this book understood what rock music was about. They embraced it, and they exemplified it. That so many of them were laid low by the perils beneath rock's thrilling power fails to negate their accomplishments or the potency of the music itself. In the words of a sage: *It is what it is*. Rock stardom takes its passengers to the pinnacle of existence. And sometimes it dashes them back down again before they can do anything about it.

Essential Listening

Throughout this book we offer "Essential Listening" advice—CDs that serve as introductions to the recorded work of rock's casualties. Recommendations are based on recordings in print in the United States in early 2001. Expensive boxed sets and multidisc sets are generally overlooked in favor of greatest-hits collections more accessible to newcomers. In some cases additional recordings have been listed for listeners who might want to dig deeper into an artist's catalogue.

But You Forgot . . .

Casualties of Rock attempts to cover a broad overview of rock 'n' roll's history of death, tragedy, and misfortune. The selection process to determine who was included in the book was, at times, cause for debate. The "What is rock 'n' roll?" philosophical question involves a level of semantic exploration that was largely avoided. Indisputable country, blues, and jazz artists were omitted in order to limit the field to rockers. Two hip-hop artists were included after deciding their stories and music represent an essential component of contemporary rock. One nonmusician was included on the basis of his vitality to music history. And three still-living musicians were picked for the book, based on the crucial nature of their stories to understanding the pitfalls of the rock-star life. Surely any knowledgeable reader of this book will dispute the choices made—some rockers were included, for instance, who died of natural causes rather than through vice or mishap, and several artists were certainly more pop than rock 'n' roll. The overriding goal of *Casualties of Rock* was to capture as many essential stories as possible, in a way that narrates their lives and their relevance to rock history. Readers might agree to disagree on choices they would have made differently.

G. G. Allin

"When I Die"

Rock 'n' roll has always coveted the power to shock, but G. G. Allin operated on a level of vile sleaze that was all his own. His stage performances involved attacking and fighting his audiences, stripping nude, cutting himself, and smearing himself with excrement. His music was unlistenable, amateurish noise that plumbed the depths of wretched bigotry and hatred. Album titles included *Freaks, Faggots, Drunks & Junkies* and the astutely titled *America's Most Hated*.

Allin inevitably gained a form of perverse notoriety, and recorded and toured well into the eighties. His insane behavior caught up with him, though, and he was imprisoned for several years. After being released in 1993, Allin hit the road. For much of his career he had promised to kill himself onstage, but instead he succumbed to a heroin overdose on June 28, 1993. The artist who had made it his life's work to be the most repulsive, loathsome, lowdown rocker in history had accomplished all he had set out to do, and is no more.

1956–1993

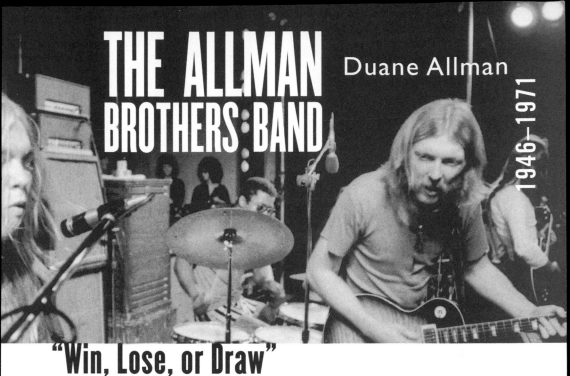

THE ALLMAN BROTHERS BAND

Duane Allman

1946–1971

"Win, Lose, or Draw"

They liked their hair long and their amplifiers turned up loud—all the better to hear their soaring, ascending dual guitar leads. They were certainly no lightweights when it came to drinking and non-prescription pharmaceutical usage. And if they didn't laugh in the face of death, they certainly brushed the Grim Reaper aside and carried on with their business.

With a history that comprises equal doses of calamity and discord alleviated by bursts of creative brilliance, southern pioneers the Allman Brothers Band represent one of the more lively ongoing dramas in rock 'n' roll. Their multiple incarnations and tendency to lose band members to untimely deaths has granted them a morbidly legendary status that at times threatens to eclipse their position as inspirational forefathers. By century's end, they had somehow kept the torch aloft via relentless touring.

Gregg and Duane Allman began playing together while still in their teens in Daytona Beach, Florida; Gregg sang and played keyboards and guitar, while Duane demonstrated an almost supernatural proficiency on the fretboard. After various incarnations (including the confection-referencing Allman Joys), they formed the Hourglass in 1967. Two albums later they were back to square one, and Duane

decamped for session work that included a residency at Fame Studios in Muscle Shoals, where he played on records by Wilson Pickett, Percy Sledge, King Curtis, and Aretha Franklin.

Duane's career as a session man would continue throughout his life—he would play with Boz Scaggs, Otis Rush, Laura Nyro, and most famously on Eric Clapton's Derek and the Dominos release *Layla*—but in the meantime he returned to collaborating with his brother. Spare parts were assembled from Gregg's band, the Second Coming (Dickey Betts on guitar, Berry Oakley on bass), and drummer Butch Trucks from a previous band called the 31st of February. A final component was Muscle Shoals drummer Jai Johanny Johanson. Perhaps befuddled by the variety of names under which they had worked in the past, the new assembly of players played it straight and dubbed itself the Allman Brothers Band.

The Allmans released a self-titled debut in 1969 that escaped significant chart notice but began to cause a commotion in their native South. A second LP, *Idlewild South*, cracked the U.S. Top 40 the next year. The Allman Brothers Band were developing a distinctive, soulful sound that meshed traditional roots music with free-form instrumental explorations that featured twin dueling guitar leads. It was onstage that they became more than the sum of their

Berry Oakley
1948–1972

Lamar Williams
1947–1983

in 1975, when Gregg was "invited" to testify against him—under threat of a grand-jury indictment if he refused. Gregg, trapped in a bad situation, complied. The other Allmans took exception to this breach of esprit de corps, particularly when Herring was sentenced to seventy-five years in prison. By 1976 the Allman Brothers Band decided it would be best to pursue other projects.

In 1977, Gregg Allman marked a tumultuous marriage to Cher by releasing the terrible *Two the Hard Way*, credited to "Allman and Woman." By 1979 Gregg and Cher were divorced and a reunited Allman Brothers Band released the Top 10 *Enlightened Rogues*. The band split again a couple of years later, and tragedy struck once more in 1983, when Lamar Williams died of cancer linked to his exposure to Agent Orange during the Vietnam War. Members pursued side projects until the inevitable Allman Brothers reunion in 1989—by 1991 they were named "Comeback of the Year" in *Rolling Stone*. The group toured like old warhorses throughout the nineties and demonstrated an admirable willingness to release new material to a marketplace in which their music was no longer in fashion.

In 2000 there was another Allman-related casualty when Allen Woody, former bassist in a latter-day Allmans incarnation, was found dead in a New York City hotel. Later that same year the group reached an acrimonious turning point when Dickey Betts was fired from the Allmans after thirty years of guitar slinging; Betts reportedly entered a rehab center soon after. The Allmans were fictionalized in Cameron Crowe's film *Almost Famous* later in 2000; the fictional band Stillwater, depicted in the movie as exemplars of seventies rockin' excess, was based at least in part on the Allman Brothers Band.

Drugs, jail, death, betrayal. Fate has thrown them all at the Allman Brothers, and more. And at the turn of the century, they were still ticking.

parts, developing a fierce interplay and quality set list. In 1971 they released a live recording, *At Fillmore East*. It was a Top 10 hit and installed the group as one of America's premiere rock 'n' roll acts.

But the Allmans were beset by tragedy almost immediately. Four days after *At Fillmore East* was certified gold, Duane Allman was coming home after wishing Berry Oakley's wife a happy birthday in Macon, Georgia. Riding his motorcycle home, he lost control while swerving to avoid a truck. He died after three hours of emergency surgery.

The band carried on, releasing the Top 5 *Eat a Peach* early in 1972 (it contained Duane's last recorded work). In November that year, though, the Allman Brothers' resilience was tested again when Berry Oakley crashed his motorcycle into a bus and was killed. His accident occurred in Macon, a scant three blocks from the site of Duane Allman's wreck a year earlier. The band carried on with Lamar Williams taking Oakley's place on bass.

Instead of giving up after suffering two tragedies in two years, the resilient Allmans responded to adversity by topping their previous commercial success. The 1973 LP *Brothers and Sisters* topped the charts, and Dickey Betts's song "Ramblin' Man" rose to #2 and became the band's signature tune. Tours and spin-off projects continued into the mid-seventies; then the plot began to unravel badly. The Allmans' former road manager and bodyguard, John "Scooter" Herring, stood trial for drug trafficking

ESSENTIAL LISTENING
A Decade of Hits 1969–1979
At Fillmore East
Idlewild South

ROCK AND ROLL HALL OF FAME
Inducted 1995

BADFINGER

Tom Evans
1947–1983

Peter Ham
1947–1975

"No Dice"

British pop band Badfinger started off with a blaze of good fortune, earning the support of the Beatles for their inaugural efforts. But after an initial run of success, the band was dogged by financial and management problems that would undermine their ability to record and remain intact. Eventually two of Badfinger's founding members committed suicide in the same manner, tragically at wit's end over the run of awful luck the group was forced to suffer. Perhaps the most lamentable aspect of Badfinger's hard-luck story is that their travails have overshadowed their knack for a catchy single and their deceptively easygoing postpsychedelic pop.

After a name change from the Iveys, Badfinger signed on with the Beatles's Apple Records in 1968; Paul McCartney lent hands-on support to their work on the soundtrack to

Peter Sellers's *The Magic Christian*, and gave them a song to record. The resultant "Come and Get It" placed in the Top 10. Thus began a short run of finely crafted pop hits including "No Matter What" and "Day After Day." Badfinger songwriters Peter Ham and Tom Evans collaborated on the composition "Without You," which was a #1 single in 1972 for singer Harry Nilsson. Badfinger had a bent for radio-friendly tunes that nicely fit the sound of the times. In 1972 the group seemed poised for a lengthy career.

But by the next year things started to change. The band's alliance with the Beatles had helped them at first, but the Fab Four's shadow was long and difficult to escape. Badfinger's final release for Apple, the anatomically designated *Ass*, stalled without reaching the Top 100. In 1974 Badfinger released an eponymous LP for Warner Bros., then the follow-up album *Wish You Were Here*; hopes of a comeback were dashed, though, when Warner claimed that $600,000 was missing from a band escrow account. *Wish You Were Here* was pulled from store shelves until the conflict was resolved. Badfinger's hopes of turning things around were effectively quashed, and the band entered into protracted disputes with their business manager over how affairs had been handled.

It was a dark time for a group that had showed so much promise; for all their success and sales, the band saw nothing in the immediate future but more struggle. In 1975 Badfinger had started work on a new LP when Peter Ham hung himself in the garage of his London home. He had reportedly been despondent over the band's business and management problems. Badfinger, for the moment, was finished.

Tom Evans was working as a pipe insulator in 1978 when he re-formed Badfinger with original and new members. The resultant LP, *Airwaves*, was not a smash but did chart. Another album fared about as well in 1981, but by this time Badfinger's quagmire of legal and business hassles had raised its ugly head again. Tom Evans was particularly distressed by his inability to access royalties from his days with Apple and for "Without You," and felt as though all his efforts

over the past decade had come to nothing. The fact is, Badfinger had produced enough successful music that only sheer management malevolence or inexcusable bungling could account for the mess that was their business affairs. In 1983, Evans committed suicide in the same manner as had bandmate Ham. Various forms of Badfinger continue to appear occasionally, but they are by definition different beasts from the band at its peak.

Badfinger's story remains one of the saddest and most unnecessarily tragic in rock 'n' roll history. Musicians and business mix badly and tend to produce explosive results—in Badfinger's case, they failed to adequately watch over the people they'd hired to watch over their money. The fact that these problems led to two suicides is one of the great tragedies of rock 'n' roll.

 **ESSENTIAL LISTENING**
The Very Best of Badfinger

The Band

were never easy to comprehend at a glance or a single listen. They were sophisticated musicians who looked as though they had stepped out of some backwoods shanty; they played music that struck with its informality as much as its cohesiveness; and they were mostly Canadians who were steeped in the history of Americana. They endured off and on for nearly three full decades, losing one member to suicide and another to a premature death in his sleep. Along the way they left a sometimes confounding but more often brilliant legacy.

Members of the Band had been playing together since the fifties, when they backed "Canadian Elvis" Ronnie Hawkins; this early rock apprenticeship ended in 1963, when Hawkins was jettisoned from the band he fronted. The Hawks continued to work together, and, in 1965, they were hired to play with Bob Dylan. They were on the ground floor when Dylan plugged in his guitar and moved to rock 'n' roll. The Band were somewhat taken aback by their place in this groundbreaking moment in rock history—up until then, they had been used to playing clubs and bars for good-time crowds. For a time in 1965 they faced portions of Dylan's audience who wanted only folk music, and who were disposed to skepticism if not outright scorn.

Dylan flamed out and wrecked his motorcycle in 1966; he went into a period of seclusion with his family near Woodstock, New York. The Band followed, setting up camp in a nearby house. Dylan came by frequently, and the musicians jammed on standards and original compositions. In the process they developed a new kind of music—knowing yet willingly naive, traditional yet hard, and driven by the fact that nearly everyone in the Band was capable of writing a killer tune. Lead vocals were alternately handled by drummer Levon Helm, bass player Rick Danko, and keyboard player Richard Manuel. Guitarist Robbie Robertson was a prolific songwriter, and multi-instrumentalist Garth Hudson held his own. The Band's collective

ROCK AND ROLL HALL OF FAME
Inducted 1994

Richard Manuel
1945–1986

Rick Danko
1943–1999

"Northern Lights—Southern Cross"

sound housed several distinctive voices and styles, and they were capable of sounding like a different group entirely from one song to the next.

The recordings from the Woodstock days would be released almost ten years later as *The Basement Tapes*, and remain as enigmatic as ever. The Band sounded at times like a bunch of grumpy old men with an archival knowledge of American music history; at the time, they were all in their twenties. Dylan on these recordings sounds like a genuine band member rather than a front man, and his vision of American music blended with the Band's to create a sound that was not of its time. It sounded like nothing less than a viable update of the primordial American soul.

In 1968 the Band released *Music from Big Pink*—named to immortalize the house they shared. It established the Band as a mysterious presence in rock 'n' roll, although it never sold in numbers commensurate with its legend. A follow-up, named simply *The Band,* matched the high standard of the group's debut and was a commercial success. The classic singles "Up on Cripple Creek" and "The Night They Drove Ol' Dixie Down" received ample radio airplay, and sounded like nothing before or since. The group toured and began to indulge in rock 'n' roll–style excess. They were a great band who managed to both sell records and earn lavish critical acclaim. The world was theirs.

The cracks appeared early on. Robbie Robertson began to dominate songwriting credits on the Band's LPs, to the chagrin of other members. The inevitable fatigue of life on the road, coupled with substance abuse, set in hard. New records of generally excellent quality followed, but the Band began to suffer from tired legs. They reunited with Dylan for the #1 LP *Planet Waves* in 1974, then toured more than twenty cities with him that year. But two years later the Band were ready to call it a career; they played an all-star farewell concert in San Francisco on Thanksgiving Day 1976, at which Dylan, Neil Young, Joni Mitchell, Muddy Waters, and Neil Diamond appeared. The show was filmed by Martin Scorsese and released as *The Last Waltz*. After a run of artistic greatness matched by commercial accomplishment, the Band appeared to have packed it in forever.

Rock 'n' roll bands seldom enjoy tidy endings. Various members went on to solo careers and outside interests that met with relatively little success—save for Robbie Robertson, who released well-received albums and film sound-tracks, acted in movies, and continued to receive a large share of past songwriting royalties. Coincidentally, Robertson was the only Band member not on board when the group re-formed in 1983. They hit the road and reconnected with their audience, but tragedy struck when the troubled Richard Manuel committed suicide in 1986. Apparently suffering from severe depression, Manuel hung himself in his room after a gig at the Cheek to Cheek Lounge in Winter Park, Florida. Cocaine and alcohol were found in his bloodstream.

The Band went on to release a new record in 1993. Although *Jericho* failed to crack the Top 100, it was a viable effort and earned positive critical notice. Another release, *Jubilation*, followed in 1998. The Band had settled into its second incarnation, still capable of playing sold-out theaters and still mining its distinctive vein of Americana, when its numbers were thinned again in 1999 by Rick Danko's demise. Although his death was attributed to natural causes, he had been arrested in Tokyo for heroin possession two years before and had a history of substance abuse. The surviving original members of the latter-day Band were whittled down to two in number, which for the moment seems to have ended the group's long odyssey. (Any possibility of reuniting with Robertson seems remote; Robertson has long showed no interest in joining his old band again, and Helm published an auto-biography in 1993, *This Wheel's on Fire,* that outlined his resentment over Robertson's allegedly taking songwriting credit for collaborative compositions.)

You Too Could Make Music in Big Pink, Probably Not as Good as the Band's, Though
In 1995 the band's onetime house in Saugerties, New York, was put on the market. The asking price? $165,000. Information was not available regarding whether the basement was soundproofed.

ESSENTIAL LISTENING
Music from Big Pink
With Bob Dylan: *The Basement Tapes*

?

1946–

Syd Barrett

"Nobody Knows Where You Are . . ."

Syd Barrett had the looks and talent to propel Pink Floyd to the forefront of London's psychedelic rock scene in the mid-sixties. But by the time the Floyd hit success on a global scale in the early seventies, the band's original leader was long absent from the picture. Barrett had succumbed to mental illness exacerbated—if not caused—by heavy use of psychedelic drugs, his erratic behavior resulting in ejection from Pink Floyd after one album. By the time of *Dark Side of the Moon* and *The Wall*, Barrett was a virtual recluse in his family's home, unable to work and unrecognizable as his former self. His memory would haunt Pink Floyd through the next three decades, often inspiring some of its best work. Barrett himself would never be heard from again.

Raised in middle-class comfort, Syd Barrett's childhood in Cambridge, England, was by all accounts a happy one. He was bright and artistic, and his parents encouraged his interest in music. His world was shattered, though, by the sudden death of his father, Dr. Max Barrett, a police pathologist and one of Britain's most prominent experts on infant mortality. Barrett was fourteen at the time; to help him cope, his mother encouraged him to rehearse in the family living room with the various garage bands he was forming with his friends.

Her indulgence paid off. While in art school, Barrett met architecture students Roger Waters, Nick Mason, and Richard Wright. They named their band after a blues record by Pink Anderson and Floyd Council, and set about playing student gigs. Soon their sound turned distinctly psychedelic, putting disparate influences into a lysergic blender. Their stage act included trip-out light shows and often frightening sound effects. Pink Floyd were abstract, aggressive, and more than a little scary. It was apparent very quickly that theirs was to be a strange voyage.

Barrett, the band's front man, underwent a transformation into a strange, tripping rock prince. He was photogenic, he sported hippie finery and a frizzed-out hairdo, and he stared at the camera with a rock star's arrogance. He also demonstrated a knack for writing short, catchy tunes to play alongside the Floyd's freak-out live jamming. In 1967 Barrett wrote the singles "Arnold Layne" and "See Emily Play." Both placed in the Top 20 in the U.K. The debut album that followed the same year, *The Piper at the Gates of Dawn*, was uniquely strange even by the standards of psychedelia. Put together almost entirely of Barrett's compositions, the LP incorporated mysticism, British whimsy, cracked storytelling, and shimmering sound effects into a sound that still sparkles with uniqueness and imaginative audacity.

But what should have been a triumph for Pink Floyd had already begun to turn sour. Barrett was taking a lot of acid even by the standards of the day—reportedly dissolving it daily into his morning coffee—and it was having a deleterious effect on his sanity. At times he was uncommunicative, leveling the world with a cold, empty stare that unnerved those around him. He frustrated bandmates by standing onstage without moving, leaving them struggling to fill in his parts while somehow playing their own, or by interminably strumming a single disjointed chord on his electric guitar while gazing into space. Caught in the grind and feeling the pressures of incipient success, the other members of Pink Floyd quickly apprehended the fact that they couldn't carry on with Barrett in this state of mental disorganization. They didn't realize it at the time, but their leader was suffering a mental collapse from which he would never recover.

The Floyd enlisted a new guitar player named David Gilmour; for a brief time he and Syd coexisted in the band, but soon Waters, Mason, and Wright summoned up the nerve to expel their front man and former guiding force. At the time, the prevailing opinion was that Pink Floyd was finished. No one who had been around him would deny that Syd Barrett could no longer function, but few thought the reconfigured Pink Floyd roster comprised enough talent to forge a lasting career in the music business. In essence, the death watch was on for Pink Floyd.

Barrett, meanwhile, did not immediately vanish from the picture. Stories of his continued erratic behavior spread through the fan grapevine—his

A Unique Approach to a Bad Hair Day

One evening close to the end of Syd Barrett's tenure with Pink Floyd, he stalled before a concert because he was unhappy with that day's configuration of his rat's-nest psychedelic coiffure. The rest of the band took the stage, leaving Barrett alone. To solve his style problem he took out a vial of Mandrax pills, of which he was taking plenty (in the U.S. we called them Quaaludes), crushed them, mixed them with a tube of hair gel, put the whole mess on top of his head, and went onstage. A couple of songs into the show, the stage lights heated up Barrett's hair; the resultant flow gave his startled bandmates the impression that their lead singer's face was melting. Serious consideration was given to finding a replacement.

 ROCK AND ROLL HALL OF FAME
Pink Floyd inducted 1996

London flat was filled with crazies who locked him in a cupboard when he was having a bad trip, and he was still showing up weekly for his Floyd paycheck and refusing to acknowledge that he was no longer in the band. He remained in London, gave interviews to the press, and attempted a solo career with the 1970 LPs *The Madcap Laughs* and *Barrett*. The records contained flashes of the old brilliance, but they were hastily recorded and underproduced. At times on the records listeners could hear Barrett lose interest partway through a song, the tempo slackening and tightening as his focus ebbed and flowed. It was obvious that Barrett still had an artistic point of view, but the chaos in his mind precluded expressing it in a manner accessible to a wide audience. His records sounded like the work of a man having a very difficult time keeping it together.

Barrett's albums wouldn't be released in the U.S. until 1974, and after *Barrett* he declined to do any promotion, returning home to Cambridge and refusing attempts to lure him back into the public eye. In the media Barrett had played upon his "madcap" persona, alternating between lucidity and rambling abstraction, but it was now clear there was nothing amusing about his slide. He was given to dark, brooding moods, and those close to him spoke of sensing his capacity for violent rages. His return to his mother and his hometown was Barrett's tacit admission that he could no longer cope on his own.

In 1972 Barrett joined a local Cambridge band called Stars. After a couple of small gigs, the group opened for cult favorites the MC5 at the Cambridge Corn Exchange. The concert is remembered as a disaster, with the sound system malfunctioning and Barrett apparently freezing up and barely able to perform. Barrett was effectively finished as a rock star (although one fascinating account has him playing abstract jazz on guitar in a Cambridge club with Cream's Jack Bruce joining in). For the next several years Barrett would avoid the public eye, and sightings of Syd in Cambridge or London would add to his growing legend as a world-class eccentric. His personal deterioration would gradually lead to increased seclusion, and he began to gain weight. Very quickly Barrett was no longer recognizable as the handsome, camera-friendly psychedelic rock pioneer of just a few years before.

Meanwhile, Barrett's bandmates were becoming one of the biggest bands in the world. After a few moderately successful post-Syd releases, the Floyd unleashed *Dark Side of the Moon* in 1973. Barrett's shadow was all over the record with its themes of mortality, paranoia, and madness, but Pink Floyd's music had become so lush and refined that it bore almost no resemblance to the Barrett *Piper* era. *Dark Side* went on to become one of the biggest sellers in music history, and Pink Floyd became very rich and successful rock stars. Barrett looked on from the sidelines.

In 1975 Pink Floyd took on the unenviable task of recording a follow-up to *Dark Side*. The group recorded a majestic, glacial soundscape that, in some respects, trumped even its predecessor. Roger Waters composed a set of lyrics that explicitly dealt with Barrett: the sense of loss the band felt toward their old friend, the pain and fear of his madness, the wasting of his talents. The end result was a poignant tribute entitled *Wish You Were Here*.

The day before embarking on a U.S. tour, Pink Floyd was in Abbey Road studios in London finalizing the mix of the song "Shine on You Crazy Diamond" for their new record. A strange man came into the studio and began quietly examining Pink Floyd's equipment. He was obese, with a shaved head and eyebrows, wearing a white coat and shoes, and holding a white plastic bag. One by one, the band and studio team were shocked when they recognized this bizarre figure as Syd Barrett. Barrett further dismayed his old bandmates by informing them that he was ready to rejoin Pink Floyd. David Gilmour was married on that hectic day, and Barrett joined the wedding reception, reportedly frightening some of the guests with his odd appearance and behavior. It was to be the last time the members of Pink Floyd saw Syd Barrett.

In the quarter century since, Barrett has recorded no new material. He has reportedly reverted to his given name of Roger, living a quiet life of seclusion tending to his garden, reading, and painting. Some reports indicate his mental condition has improved; others say it has deteriorated. Whatever the case, it is obvious that Syd Barrett—the leader of Pink Floyd, the psychedelic visionary—is no more. In his place is a middle-aged homebody with little interest in revisiting his past. He didn't set out to become a legendary mystery, it simply worked out that way. And as for his thoughts on his old band's rise to greatness and three decades of chart-topping success . . . the world may never know.

ESSENTIAL LISTENING
With Pink Floyd: *The Piper at the Gates of Dawn*
Solo: *The Madcap Laughs*

STIV BATORS

Cleveland's native son Stivin Bator relocated to New York in the mid-seventies and gravitated to the CBGB's punk scene, joining up with the Dead Boys and releasing *Young, Loud and Snotty* in 1977. The Dead Boys were raucous purveyors of generous dollops of punk attitude, but their music wasn't very good and, after 1978's *We Have Come for Your Children,* the band dissolved.

Bators released a few marginal solo projects, then hooked up with a former member of the Damned in the early eighties. The band they formed was called the Lords of the New Church, and they mined a vein of postpunk energy combined with mid-eighties apocalyptic production. Releases such as *Is Nothing Sacred?* and *The Method to Our Madness* made a slight impact, then met their destiny in cutout bins. By this time, Bators was a renowned veteran of the punk–new wave wars, a minor celebrity, and an exemplar of all things rock. On June 5, 1990, Bators died in his sleep; he'd been in Paris cooking up new projects when he was struck by a car while on his way to meet his girlfriend, Caroline Warren. Refusing medical attention, Bators underestimated the extent of his injuries and passed away later that evening. A planned postpunk supergroup involving former members of Hanoi Rocks, Sigue Sigue Sputnik, and the Dead Boys never came to pass.

1949–1990

DENNIS
1944–1983
& CARL
1946–1998
WILSON

"God Only Knows"

The Beach Boys

O ver the course of four decades the Beach Boys have endured madness, death, and internal strife, somehow always surviving in one form or another while evolving from cutting-edge pioneers into a state-fair grandstand-filling nostalgia act. They lost brothers to drowning and to cancer, and for much of their career their fortunes depended upon Brian Wilson, a man who suffered mental instability on a scale that matched his formidable gifts. The long career of the Beach Boys has always been difficult to pin down or categorize. They reached sublime heights with the legendary *Pet Sounds* LP, yet they also indulged in the staggering deep-dish fromage of performing on the kiddie-pap TV show *Full House*. For decades fans whispered about a lost masterpiece that Brian Wilson destroyed in a fit of paranoia, and there's always been the question of what the Beach Boys might have achieved if they hadn't suffered so many casualties along the way.

Driven by abusive father Murray, the Wilson brothers—Brian, Dennis, and Carl—joined with cousin Mike Love and friend Al Jardine in the early sixties to form the Beach Boys. Their early hits evoked a mythic California that resonated in the American consciousness with the pitch-perfect precision of a tuning fork. With hits such as "Surfin' Safari," "Surfin' U.S.A.," "Fun Fun Fun," and "California Girls," the Beach Boys portrayed a California of endless gnarly waves, sun-massaged beaches, and tawny tanned girls in bikinis—in short, a youth paradise. Between 1962 and 1964, the Beach Boys enjoyed nine Top 40 hits. Their songs employed sophisticated vocal harmonies and were exquisitely crafted in the studio with Brian as producer. Brian emerged as the group's most talented songwriter and a genuine visionary.

But the flaws in the Beach Boys' edifice appeared early on. Brian suffered a nervous breakdown in 1965, caused in part by his angst about touring and by pressure from Murray

Wilson. From then on, Brian's role in the Beach Boys would essentially be to call the shots in the studio—an accommodation that effectively split the group into separate touring and recording entities, laying the foundation for a long-lasting schism. The Beach Boys enlisted Glen Campbell for a short time to replace Brian, then Bruce Johnston as a more permanent replacement for live shows.

The next year the band recorded *Pet Sounds,* which included the hits "Wouldn't It Be Nice," and "God Only Knows." In retrospect it is a lasting masterpiece, wedding the Beach Boys's trademark multilayered harmonies to a shimmering and imaginative production. But its sales were slack by Beach Boys standards, and to make matters worse the group was having increasing difficulty contending with Brian. His drug intake was prodigious, his mental state was shaky, and he was consumed with staying on top of a music business whose creative stakes had been raised considerably with the release of the Beatles's *Revolver.* In 1966 Brian spent six months in the studio recording his magnum opus "Good Vibrations," a sprawling quasi-psychedelic epic that tried to reproduce the symphonic hallucinations echoing in Brian's tortured head. The other Beach Boys might have been dismayed by Brian's megalomania and perfectionism, but they couldn't deny the results. "Good Vibrations" went to the top of the charts.

Brian then began work on a project called *Smile* in late 1966 with lyricist Van Dyke Parks, and the strain nearly did him in. Fueled by drugs, ambition, and an elusive vision of musical nirvana, Brian put the Beach Boys through the wringer, recording a series of abstract, innovative sound experiments that were in another universe entirely from the upbeat pop of "Help Me, Rhonda." Brian's behavior got weirder as recording progressed, and he sank deeper into paranoia and grandiosity. At one point he was reported to have played a piano lodged in a giant sandbox. This behavior went on for more than a year; but after a fire in the studio, Brian apparently destroyed many of the tapes he was working on in a fit of irrationality.

The Beach Boys' record company was unamused by the dearth of new material being produced, and released a compilation in 1967 called *Best of the Beach Boys.* Fissures formed within the group over their new direction—or lack thereof. Some tracks survived from the tortuous sessions, such as the hit "Heroes and Villains," which appeared on a watered-down LP called *Smiley Smile,* and the title cut of 1971's *Surf's Up.* But by then the Beach Boys had entered a new era in which Brian was no longer their lone producer and creative force. In retrospect, the other members of the band pushed Brian to the periphery in an act of self-preservation, because as the seventies progressed Brian sank deeper into mental illness and

Inside a Genius Mind
"I used to go through things, and I wondered whether things were real or not. I guess it's just another stage of development, but I do hear and see magical trips that I can turn on and off. Most people don't understand that."

—Brian Wilson

Banned in D.C.
In 1983, the Beach Boys were prevented by Secretary of the Interior James Watt from performing a Fourth of July concert at the Washington Monument. Public opinion pointed out that the Beach Boys were hardly bomb-throwing radicals, and the next year First Lady Nancy Reagan personally invited the boys to play at the Monument. Watt later resigned, neglecting to comment on whether his political downfall had been precipitated by his naive willingness to mess with the Beach Boys.

ESSENTIAL LISTENING
The Greatest Hits Vol. 1: 20 Good Vibrations
Pet Sounds

seclusion. The band, always split into camps and factions, deepened its conflicts when Jardine and Love became enthusiasts of Transcendental Meditation, contrasting with Dennis and Carl Wilson's laid-back California lifestyles. As always, Brian was caught in the middle and was largely unable to meet the challenge.

The Beach Boys were a different band without Brian at the creative center, but other members stepped forward and began writing songs of their own to beef up the LPs in light of Brian's diminished output. Meanwhile, Brian was holed up in a mansion in Bel Air, growing increasingly overweight and afflicted with depression and a fractured consciousness. His narrowed world at home included a recording studio, as well as a sandbox to play in when Brian felt like getting in touch with his inner child. The Beach Boys's albums and singles made a minor commotion on the charts, but their days at the top seemed to be over. In 1974 the compilation *Endless Summer* went platinum, reviving the group's fortunes and setting the general tone for the remainder of their career: they traded on their past, heavily emphasizing their sixties hits during a long succession of tours.

Brian wasn't the only Wilson brother to face adversity. Dennis Wilson, the only regular surfer in a band that had sung the praises of sand and sea, lived a turbulent life in the shadow of older brother Brian. In the late sixties he was dismayed to find his house occupied by a strange, charismatic, wild-eyed guitar player and his entourage of young girls. The struggling musician who frightened Dennis into temporarily leaving his own home gained notoriety soon after, when the greater world came into contact with Charles Manson and his "family." Dennis attempted to break out from the Beach Boys with the 1977 solo LP *Pacific Ocean Blue,* which contained some good material but barely grazed the Top 100. Dennis was also no stranger to drugs and booze, and the Beach Boys suffered their first casualty in 1983 when he accidentally drowned in Marina Del Rey while swimming from his boat. President Reagan granted an exception that allowed Dennis to be buried at sea.

The Beach Boys continued on as essentially a nostalgia act, releasing tracks that were sometimes composed by Brian, sometimes not. In 1988 a Brian-free Beach Boys released the #1

single "Kokomo," which while a huge success did little to make fans forget the glory days. In the same year, Brian released his first solo LP, produced and written in collaboration with his therapist, Dr. Eugene Landy. The record was hailed as a Second Coming for a long-absent genius and, although it may not have lived up to the mountainous hype, *Brian Wilson* contained a few gems such as "Love and Mercy." The general record-buying public greeted the release with a yawn of indifference. Perhaps too much time had passed, too much momentum been lost. Or maybe the Beach Boys had exploited their past too long to be taken seriously as a viable creative force—a strategy that Brian himself had reaped gains from, if not actively participated in.

The fractiousness that dawned in the sixties between Beach Boys members ignited anew in the nineties, when Mike Love filed lawsuits against Brian for defamation (based on statements in Brian's autobiography) and over a royalty dispute. The former suit was settled; Mike Love prevailed in the latter. A variety of other lawsuits was filed by and against various band members as the Beach Boys' lives became increasingly litigious and combative. Claims were bandied about that Brian was being manipulated and controlled by his therapist, rumors that Brian did little to dispel in interviews. Although Brian was back in the public eye, slimmed down and coherent, it was obvious that he was a troubled man given to deep anxiety and despair. He also felt constant pressure from his less-talented bandmates to produce new songs, to somehow re-create the glory days and keep the cash coming.

The end of the nineties saw Brian release another critically lauded solo LP, *Imagination,* to mediocre sales. The Beach Boys suffered another casualty in 1998, when Carl Wilson died of lung cancer at fifty-one. By year's end two different acts were on the road. One was "The Beach Boys: Family and Friends," featuring Jardine and various children of band members. The other was billing itself as the Beach Boys, although its sole links to the past were Love and Johnston—making it the first Beach Boys lineup without a Wilson. Finally, it seemed that mortality and Brian Wilson's tenuous peace and independence precluded any return to the glory days.

Chris Bell
"I Am the Cosmos"

Chris Bell founded seminal cult favorite Big Star in Memphis in the early seventies, along with former Box Tops singer Alex Chilton. Bell and Chilton were a potent songwriting and performing combination, and they blended their gifts on Big Star's 1972 release *#1 Record*. Few LPs have been less appropriately named, since this debut failed to graze the charts. Big Star's punchy hooks and studio precision would later typify the style called "power pop," but in 1972 there was no such thing and the sound's pioneers were pitifully rewarded for their efforts.

Bell himself was a tortured, conflicted man. He was a Bible-toting Christian, but instead of finding solace in his religion, he was racked with guilt over his drug and alcohol intake, his homosexuality, and his rock 'n' roll lifestyle. By 1973 he had left Big Star. Although he made a few uncredited contributions to the band's sophomore release *Radio City*, in the end it didn't matter much. Big Star's second release—today considered by many a classic rife with economical songwriting and knowing, impassioned performances—flopped on the charts. Bell deepened his substance abuse, and after time spent recording demos and embarking on half-hearted tours, he settled down in Memphis to manage a restaurant owned by his father.

In 1978 Bell was having another try in the studio, but after a disagreement there he got high and drove his 1977 Triumph straight into a phone pole. He died instantly. Bell's solo work would remain unreleased until 1992—fourteen years after his death. *I Am the Cosmos* revealed a lost gem of pained yearning, bittersweet beauty, and inner turmoil that found an eager audience already rediscovering Big Star. Bell's raging battle of the soul had ended long before, but his last songs had finally reached those who would care to hear them.

ESSENTIAL LISTENING
Solo: *I Am the Cosmos*
With Big Star: *#1 Record/Radio City*
(both LPs are available on a single CD)

"Metal Guru"

Marc Bolan

T. Rex front man Marc Bolan was a major star of early-seventies British glam rock whose plundering of rock 'n' roll history in combination with a theatrical stage presence in some ways mirrored David Bowie's ascension to the pop pantheon. But while Bowie's star would shine white-hot as the decade progressed, Bolan's began to ebb and turn cold. His accidental death just shy of his thirtieth birthday nullified any fading comeback hopes.

Bolan's dogged pursuit of stardom led him from an early modeling gig into music. The former Mark Feld rode the trends, playing in a skiffle group, then going mod in the early sixties. He was a stylish young man determined to make his presence felt; he appeared in mod feature pieces in the English publications *Evening Standard* and *Town*, and popped up on the *Five O'Clock Club* TV program. By 1965 he was recording as Toby Tyler, a name that he soon abandoned in favor of the less alliterative Marc Bolan.

The days of mod were numbered in Britain, and Bolan astutely latched onto the next big thing: flower power. He joined the psychedelic band John's Children in 1967, then that summer auditioned applicants to form a group of his own. Steve Peregrin Took joined Bolan to form the nucleus of Tyrannosaurus Rex. Their first album bore the economical title *My People Were Fair and Had Sky in Their Hair But Now They're Content to Wear Stars on Their Brows*. The early work Tyrannosaurus Rex mined was a mixture of blissed-out hippiedom and British whimsy that also reflected in their next album title: *Prophets, Seers and Sages, The Angels of the Ages*.

Looking back, this was hardly lasting stuff. But the albums achieved U.K. Top 20 status at the time, and Bolan developed a following. His voice was a bit reedy, but it contained a signature tone that was distinctly his own. His curly-haired

ESSENTIAL LISTENING
Cosmic Dancer (compilation)
Electric Warrior

HE SAID IT

"I was living in a twilight world of drugs, booze, and kinky sex."

—Marc Bolan

good looks were also being favorably compared to angels in Botticelli paintings, which didn't hurt his odds of achieving greater fame.

By 1969, Took was gone and times were changing. After an unsuccessful U.S. tour, Bolan saw that the age of the hippie was coming to a close. Bolan started playing electric guitar on records by T. Rex, a shortened band name adopted in 1970. The same year would see Bolan playing guitar on David Bowie's "The Prettiest Star" single and the release of "Ride a White Swan," which charted #2 U.K. and was T. Rex's first U.S. Top 100 hit.

The next year Bolan went on a winning streak. It was the dawning of glam rock in Britain, and Ziggy Stardust was a year away from being hatched from the musty corners of Bowie's unconscious. Bolan actually got there first, matching surreal sexual imagery with crunching guitar riffs, an androgynous, prettified image, and an outrageous stage presence. The hits started coming: "Hot Love," "Jeepster," "Bang a Gong (Get It On)," "Telegram Sam," "Children of the Revolution." T. Rex filled arenas in Britain and hit the Top 40 in America. Bolan's music was fun, witty, and capable of inciting wanton behavior in youth on both sides of the Atlantic. In short, Marc Bolan experienced about two years of greatness.

Then things started to dry up. When Bowie conquered the U.K. and then became a big star in America—something Bolan had failed to do—Marc saw his fortunes slide. Bolan's music still charted, but sales and chart position began a swift slide even at home in Britain. His music simply wasn't as good as it had been a year or two before. Bolan himself was living a dissolute rock 'n' roll lifestyle that hardly nourished his muse. Having spent his short life in pursuit of stardom, Bolan seemed to lose track of what had got him there.

Still, Bolan didn't disappear completely. He had a U.K. Top 20 hit in 1976 with "I Love to Boogie," but the next year two of T. Rex's singles failed to trouble the charts. Bolan served as a guest columnist for England's *Record Mirror* and hosted a short-lived weekday-afternoon TV show called *Marc*. Bolan by this time was haggard and exhausted from his lifestyle and the pressure of watching his fame slip away. David Bowie appeared on the *Marc* program, a poignant moment in which the former king of U.K. glam, spent and out of ideas, was reduced to exploiting the onetime acolyte who was promoting a new LP ("Heroes") that would leave an indelible mark on rock music. The shortened performance went badly, with Bowie suffering an electric shock and Bolan tumbling off the soundstage.

Bolan was romantically involved with Gloria Jones, an American soul singer who served in Bolan's band and was a successful songwriter; the two had a son in 1975. A week after Bowie's appearance on the *Marc* show, Bolan and Gloria went out for a long night of clubbing in London. At five the next morning, Gloria Jones drove their car into a tree. She was badly hurt, and Marc Bolan died. His thirtieth birthday was two weeks later. In 1980 Steve Peregrin Took, cofounder of Tyrannosaurus Rex, devoted a royalty check to the purchase of morphine and magic mushrooms; his throat numbed by the mushrooms, Took subsequently choked to death on a cherry. Steve Currie, bass player during T. Rex's charmed run of hits, died the next year in a car accident in Portugal.

Bolan had a short run of success, and he left behind a clutch of great songs that sound superb more than twenty years later. Bolan's signature style was heard again in 1994, when Oasis borrowed a very T. Rex–sounding riff for their British hit "Cigarettes and Alcohol." In 1997, on the twentieth anniversary of his death, Bolan's son and brother dedicated a stone memorial near the site of Marc's demise.

Tommy Bolin

Sioux City, Iowa's own Tommy Bolin firmly established a pattern of replacing hard-rock riffmeisters in established bands before he succumbed at an early age to the rock 'n' roll lifestyle. Dropping out of high school after a battle over the length of his hair—he apparently preferred it long—Bolin went to Denver and plied his guitarist's trade in now forgotten hard-rock bands.

Bolin's fortunes improved in 1973, when former James Gang guitarist and future Eagle Joe Walsh gave him a job recommendation; Bolin subsequently wrote for and performed on two James Gang albums that marked the band's commercial decline. After a solo project, Bolin was tapped on the shoulder in 1975 to replace notoriously prickly Ritchie Blackmore in Deep Purple. He played on the Spinal Tap–influenced *Come Taste the Band*; Deep Purple broke up the next year. Bolin released another solo LP, *Private Eyes*, and was on the road promoting it when he died of an accidental drug overdose in his Miami hotel room.

1951–1976

1948–1911

 ROCK AND ROLL HALL OF FAME
Led Zeppelin inducted 1995

JOHN
BONHAM

"NO QUARTER"

Best remembered as the driving force behind the Sturm und Drang that was Led Zeppelin's groundbreaking fury, drummer John Bonham was an unholy behemoth behind the kit. Listening today to "Whole Lotta Love" it's almost impossible to imagine any human drummer producing such percussive thunder. Bonham was instrumental to Led Zeppelin's reinvention of hard rock, as well as their well-earned status as a four-headed monster of the road (five-headed if one counts manager Peter Grant). They were no strangers to the temptations of libation and assorted mood-altering substances, and John Bonham's own ferocious propensity for the bottle led to his early death and the end of Led Zeppelin.

John Bonham had played in a Birmingham group called Band of Joy with singer Robert Plant; when Plant was tapped to sing for renowned guitarist Jimmy Page's post-Yardbirds project, Plant in turn recommended his old friend. After a tour under the name New Yardbirds, the band opted for the oxymoronic appellation Led Zeppelin. They received instant attention due to Page's pedigree in the Yardbirds and years of high-profile session work, and followed through with recordings that wedded Plant's banshee wailing to Page's increasingly virtuosic blues-based guitar. Beneath it all was the rumbling monumental racket of Bonham's drums: he played fast, he played hard, he played with extraordinary deftness and energy. The band's second LP, challengingly titled *Led Zeppelin II*, was a #1 smash in the U.S. (the first of five chart straddlers) and featured the drum workout "Moby Dick," subsequently a live staple.

Led Zeppelin were the most popular rock band of their day, and they regularly released hit albums and undertook marauding tours of sold-out venues. They became fabulously wealthy and indulged their various appetites with little regard for reason or propriety. They lived like they sounded: hard, with breakneck speed, unbridled lust, and giving no quarter along the way. By the end of the seventies Zeppelin's momentum was somewhat stalled, but they could still sell out any arena and even lesser LPs were #1 hits. A window into Bonham's life off the road was afforded in the 1976 concert film *The Song Remains the Same*, which included a vignette of Bonham proudly showing his country estate and fleet of vintage cars.

Bonham's alcohol intake—always prodigious—became a problem in 1980, when he fell ill after three songs at a concert in Nuremberg. The band decided to soldier on, and met at Page's home in September of that year to get into fighting shape for a projected American tour. It wouldn't come to pass; Bonham went on a binge and was found dead in Page's home after passing out and choking to death on his own vomit. In December the band released a statement saying that Led Zeppelin was breaking up. There was no way to imagine Zeppelin carrying on without the beating heart of Bonham's drums.

ESSENTIAL LISTENING
Led Zeppelin II (one of the all-time great rock drum LPs)
Houses of the Holy

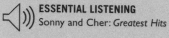

Sonny Bono

1935–1998

"A Cowboy's Work Is Never Done"

Detroit-born Salvatore Bono—let's call him Sonny—lived out a unique odyssey in the public eye that spanned four decades and took him from the considerable weirdness of Phil Spector's musical laboratory to the considerable weirdness of the U.S. Congress. His was a tireless engine that continued running long after his public marriage and divorce to Cher and his subsequent failed solo career. His death in a skiing accident reminded millions that, in the end, he was a charming, funny guy many grew up with while basking in the cathode-ray glow of TV.

Bono began writing songs in his teens, and by the early sixties was trying to break into the music business with little success until the Searchers recorded his "Needles and Pins"; it was a Top 20 hit in 1964. The same year Sonny also struck gold when he married Cherilyn Sarkasian LaPier, a young woman more than a decade his junior whom he met in a coffee shop and helped become a studio backup singer for Sonny's new employer, legendary genius and sometime crackpot Phil Spector.

Sonny had a vision of stepping out from behind the anonymity of for-hire songwriting and performing his own compositions with his new wife. He dubbed them Caesar and Cleo—it must have seemed right at the time—and they recorded a couple of singles that went nowhere. In 1965 they decided to go with the obvious, calling themselves Sonny and Cher. That same year they released "I Got You Babe," a Bono composition that went to #1 and instantly established the duo as stars. Bono dressed himself and Cher in outrageous hippie regalia and generally set about a relentless course of promotion and recording—all orchestrated by Bono himself. More Top 10 hits followed, including "Baby Don't Go," and "The Beat Goes On." It was lightweight fare, and neither Sonny nor Cher had a great voice, but their straightforward pop found an audience. Although by decade's end their act was wearing thin, Sonny and Cher worked Vegas and achieved some chart success in the early seventies.

It was in 1971 that Sonny and Cher began their second incarnation as TV stars; *The Sonny and Cher Comedy Hour* debuted in 1971 and was a smash. It was a variety show that relied heavily on jokes and innuendoes about Sonny and Cher's marriage, with Sonny eagerly playing the part of stooge/fall guy to Cher's elegant, disdainful siren. Audiences lapped it up, and the show ran until 1974. That same year, though, Cher filed for divorce from Sonny and embarked on an ill-considered marriage with Gregg Allman mere days after the finalization of the split. Sonny and Cher reconvened for another variety show in 1976, but the magic was essentially gone. Both former partners attempted subsequent TV shows and solo careers. Cher met with mixed success until a resurgence in the eighties as an actress. Bono failed to sustain a viable career in the music business, and by 1983 he had opened a restaurant in Los Angeles.

But Sonny Bono wasn't finished. In 1988, after moving to Palm Springs, he registered to vote for the first time in his life and announced his candidacy for mayor. He won. His appetite whetted for public office, Bono set upon the political world with the same zeal he'd evinced in the music industry. In 1994, following an unsuccessful bid in 1992, Republican Sonny Bono won a California congressional seat in the U.S. House of Representatives by a 56-to-38-percent margin. Those who remembered him as a TV fall guy were surprised by the seriousness and energy he brought to his new role.

On January 5, 1998, this new chapter suddenly ended. While on a ski vacation with his family, Bono struck a tree next to an intermediate skiing trail at the Heavenly Ski Resort in South Lake Tahoe. Bono had been skiing alone and had been missing for several hours when his body was discovered by the ski patrol; a coroner's report indicated that he had died instantly. Bono's widow, Mary, subsequently assumed his congressional seat.

Please, Don't Sugar-Coat It
"Politicians don't work for the people; the system works for the politicians. It's a huge crime to be so greedy and to let the people down and the country fall apart. Politicians are one step below used-car salesmen."

—Cher, in THE WASHINGTON POST following Sonny Bono's congressional victory

D. BOON

1958–1985

"Life as a Rehearsal"

The early eighties witnessed the rise of hard-core punk bands such as Black Flag and Hüsker Dü who represented a shot of dirty black coffee in contrast to the decaf sound of MTV-sanctioned new wave. Joining the class was southern California's Minutemen, who enjoyed a run of revolutionary punk experimentation before their leader died in a van accident that effectively terminated the band.

Dennes Dale Boon—known as D. Boon in his recording and playing days—formed the Minutemen with bassist Mike Watt in hardscrabble San Pedro, California. They named the group after their songs—short, intense bursts of ambitious noise—and as a tongue-in-cheek reference to right-wing militarism. The Minutemen were in fact staunch leftists who played punk with an experimental twist, incorporating funk, folk, and jazz into their incendiary stew. In 1980 they recorded an EP for the seminal record label SST, home to many crucial American punk bands and an early exemplar of the anticorporate indie sensibility.

In 1984 the Minutemen recorded *Double Nickels on the Dime*, a politically charged double album that remains a classic of its time. The Minutemen were little known to mainstream audiences but enjoyed a spike in visibility the next year, when they toured as opening act for R.E.M. Boon and company were a rousing live act, capable of insane abrasion one moment and poetic transcendence the next. The burly Boon became known as one of the rising stars of the American underground rock scene. His tantalizing talent was silenced, though, on December 23, 1985, when he was killed while traveling between shows in Arizona. Mike Watt went on to an enduring indie-rock career, both as a solo artist and with his subsequent band fIREHOSE.

Tim Buckley
1947–1975

the Buckleys

"Last Goodbye"

The two Buckleys—father and son—did not know each other. Tim's recording career lasted almost a decade while his son managed to complete only one studio album. Had they not been related, had they not shared the same surname, they would never have been mentioned in the same breath. But Tim and Jeff Buckley were father and son, and their inexorable ties of blood were tragically strengthened by the strange, accidental deaths they both suffered while still young men.

Tim Buckley was playing clubs in L.A. in the mid-sixties when he was spotted by Herb Cohen, Frank Zappa's manager. Cohen arranged a gig for Buckley at New York's Night Owl; Buckley was immediately offered a record deal, and his eponymous debut hit the stores three months later. Tim's early style mixed folk and rock, but the most interesting element of his music was his voice—versatile and emotive, memorable after one hearing. Tim became a respected figure in rock circles, both for his performing and for his songwriting, and in 1969 he enjoyed his highest U.S. chart success (#81) with *Happy Sad*, which found Tim employing jazzy arrangements and elements of free-form song structure. His music was complex and sophisticated, and his voice continued to develop as a multifaceted instrument.

Following *Happy Sad*, Buckley moved from one record label to another and for a time pursued a more avant-garde direction. Such releases as 1970's *Lorca* and the next year's *Starsailor* featured a free-jazz direction that was largely unwelcomed by an audience awaiting a new set of solid songs. Tim backed off recording for a time, doing cameos in movies and working as a chauffeur. In 1972 he released *Greetings from L.A.*, which represented yet another stylistic departure—this time into funky, rhythmic territory. The record had its merits but nimbly evaded the charts, as did Buckley's next two releases. It seemed that he was trapped in a cycle of diminishing returns.

In 1975 Tim returned to the road for the first time in several years. He entertained ambitious plans for a live retrospective, and for writing a novel and screenplay; none of this came to pass. On June 29, Tim Buckley died in Santa Monica of an overdose of heroin and morphine. Most accounts have Buckley succumbing after snorting a line of white powder that he mistook for cocaine; in the liner notes for 1990's *Dream Letter (Live in London, 1968)*, Buckley's guitarist Lee Underwood maintains that Tim died because his recently cleaned-up metabolism was unable to absorb the amount of heroin he had consumed. A friend would be convicted of involuntary manslaughter for supplying Tim with the drugs that ended his life.

Jeff Buckley was eight at the time, the product of a brief affair in the mid-sixties that ended with Tim leaving behind his girlfriend and son. Though Jeff would downplay links with his father in later years, one imagines he felt the anguish of never knowing his father following

Tim's accidental demise in California. But by all reports, Jeff's daily life had nothing at all to do with Tim Buckley. He grew up musically talented, and by high school he was playing in bands. He played jazz and reggae in L.A., then moved to New York and assumed membership in the short-lived Gods and Monsters. Jeff's talent seemed to explode exponentially in his early twenties; he developed a solo act playing clubs and cafes, and his reputation quickly grew as a phenomenal talent gifted with a voice of soaring range and dynamics. Soon enough he had a record deal.

Jeff released *Live at Sin-é* in 1993, a document of his small-club act, but it was with the release of 1994's *Grace* that he became a star of sorts. He recorded his songs with a full band, employing open tunings, bombastic highs, and imaginative arrangements that earned comparisons to Led Zeppelin's "Kashmir" and Pakistan's legendary Nusrat Fateh Ali Khan. At the center of this sonic terrain was his voice—impossibly strong, rich, with a vertiginous cosmic quality that was at times strikingly reminiscent of his father's. *Grace* was not a huge commercial hit, but it was acknowledged as a stunning first effort—some called it one of the greatest debut releases in rock 'n' roll history—and earned some airplay with the single "Last Goodbye."

Jeff didn't return to the recording studio until 1997, when he began work in Memphis on a project that had suffered gestational fits and starts. He had laid down some early tracks when, on May 29, he and a friend went to the local Mud Island Harbor. Jeff decided he wanted to take a swim and jumped into the Mississippi River with all his clothes on, including his boots. Within minutes he disappeared. The police were called, but Jeff's body wasn't located until June 4, when he was found floating near the city's Beale Street district. Recordings from the Memphis sessions were released in 1998 as *Sketches (For My Sweetheart the Drunk)*; in 2000, *Mystery White Boy,* a collection of live recordings, was compiled by Jeff's mother and his band.

Talk of a curse that passed from father to son amounts to disrespect for their memory; it's sufficient to say that both young men took chances that ended their lives in a fairly arbitrary and random manner. Tim Buckley's recording career, from all appearances, was nearly finished by the time of his death. Jeff's was just beginning—what survives from the 1997 Memphis sessions is vital and intriguing. These two talented men were in life linked by name only. But, in death, they will inevitably be remembered in the father and son roles they never played in real life.

Remembering a Complicated Legacy

"I knew [Tim Buckley] for a total of nine days. The people that did know him apparently have magic memories of him, but it's been a claustrophobic thing all my life. I guess my dad and I were born with the same parts, like some people are born with the same bone structure, but it's not his voice ... it's not even my voice, it's the voice that has been passed on through the male Buckley family. His father sang, my grandmother sang too. My uncle could sing his ass off."

—Jeff Buckley

Jeff Buckley
1966–1997

Music fans tend to remember the first time they heard the crunchy stew that is Metallica. In the early eighties, beginning with the release *Kill 'Em All*, the band revolutionized heavy metal and earned itself a lasting place in rock history. First there was the sound—heavier than heavy, with epic slabs of guitar and whiplash-inducing tempo shifts. Then the lyrics—slashing out like lightning from black storm-clouds, tackling war, death, and injustice with an intelligent, articulated rage as startling as it was stirring.

Holding down the bass in Metallica's early incarnation was Cliff Burton, a longhaired, head-banging metal monster of the first order. A lasting image from the time is Burton's lowered head bashing at the air in time with the music, as though he were trying to smash through some invisible wall. Metallica suffered a painful casualty in 1986 in Sweden; the group's tour bus slid off an ice-slicked road, and Burton was pinned underneath the wreckage and killed. Metallica soon regrouped with new bassist Jason Newsted and found its greatest commercial success in the nineties.

 **ESSENTIAL LISTENING**
Metallica: *Kill 'Em All*

1962–1986

CLIFF BURTON

KAREN
CARPENTER
"Rainy Days and Mondays"

1950–1983

ESSENTIAL LISTENING
The Carpenters: *Singles 1969–1981*
Love Songs (compilation)

In the early seventies the Carpenters released a series of hit singles and LPs that dominated the charts and incensed hipster counterculturalists everywhere. At the core of the Carpenters's feather-light pop was the deceptively world-weary voice of young Karen Carpenter, a singer of great natural gifts who attained stardom by the age of twenty. Her decade in the limelight wasn't a happy one, however, and the devastating effects of anorexia nervosa killed her after a painful and lengthy struggle.

Karen's brother Richard was, initially, the musical shining star of the Carpenter siblings; he studied classical piano at Yale and in his late teens founded a jazz group for which he enlisted Karen on drums. By the late sixties the pair had formed a vocal group called Spectrum. For the moment, fame was not calling. But they didn't have long to wait.

The Carpenters recorded demo tapes that would be the blueprint for their subsequent work—ornate pop with lush arrangements and Karen's increasingly accomplished vocals firmly at the fore. A&M Records's Herb Alpert got a copy of the tape, and the Carpenters nabbed a record contract in 1969. The next year they had their first #1 single with "Close to You."

And with that began a run of pop successes that made the Carpenters one of the most ubiquitous groups of the early seventies. Hits included "We've Only Just Begun," "For All We Know," "Superstar," "Top of the World," and "Please Mr. Postman." By 1975 the Carpenters had placed a dozen singles in the U.S. Top 10. Karen was famous, wealthy, and on top of her game. But that same year she and Richard were forced to cancel a world tour when Karen was diagnosed with severe exhaustion and forced to stay in her bed. The troubled soul that lived behind Karen Carpenter's squeaky-clean disguise was now impossible to ignore, and she began years of struggle with anorexia nervosa.

During the late seventies Richard Carpenter developed a Quaalude addiction and sought treatment. Karen by then was locked into the agonizing struggles of being anorexic, starving herself, exercising to excess, using laxatives, and bulimic vomiting. The Carpenters were largely absent from the charts, but managed to maintain a public presence via television specials. Friends and family, meanwhile, were becoming increasingly alarmed by Karen's weight loss.

Carpenter struggled to regain her health, and married in 1980. The relationship lasted only a year, though, and she subsequently moved to New York to seek treatment for her condition. By 1982 she seemed to be turning a corner; though she was still emaciated, she had put on weight and seemed optimistic. She returned to her parents' home in Downey, California, for the holidays. On February 4, Carpenter's mother found Karen collapsed on a bedroom floor. By the time they reached the hospital, Karen was dead. The coroner ruled that she had died of "heartbeat irregularities brought on by chemical imbalances associated with anorexia nervosa."

In their time the Carpenters were reviled in some circles as the personification of suburban sterility and wholesome blandness. Richard Nixon invited them to visit the White House in 1972 and called them "young America at Its best"—an endorsement tailor-made to elicit loathing from rock 'n' rollers in the age of Vietnam. There is no getting around the fact that the Carpenters's music and image were deeply, profoundly square. Richard and Karen were nonetheless talented purveyors of their craft, and never seemed to care much whether *Rolling Stone* was prepared to bestow upon them the mantle of artistic credibility.

In the years since Karen Carpenter's death she has become a figure of curiosity and increased respect. The made-for-TV film *The Karen Carpenter Story* aired in 1988 to high ratings. Increased awareness in recent times of anorexia nervosa has enabled fans and nonfans alike to more deeply comprehend the magnitude of suffering endured by victims of the deadly syndrome. Some have tried to appropriate Carpenter as a radical symbol of the supposed spiritual rot festering beneath suburban America, but one might wish these theorists would pick on someone else's memory, since they are probably the same people who would have scorned her image in life. Nearly twenty years after passing away, Karen Carpenter is best remembered as a talented singer and troubled woman who succumbed too young to a problem few properly understood.

Fond Memories from the Über-Hip
1994 saw the release of *If I Were a Carpenter*, a tribute album featuring interpretations of Carpenters hits by Sheryl Crow, Sonic Youth, Shonen Knife, Babes in Toyland, Matthew Sweet, and Cracker.

Harry Chapin

"ON THE ROAD TO KINGDOM COME"

1942–1981

playing local clubs and making documentaries with his brothers. A 1969 film called *Legendary Champions*, made by Chapin with Jim Jacobs, was nominated for an Oscar. Always a driven workaholic, by 1971 Chapin had honed his stage act sufficiently to garner a record deal; at the time he employed an innovative setup, matching his acoustic guitar and voice with bass and cello.

Chapin wrote narrative "message" songs—not everyone's choice. Chapin was routinely smacked about by critics, but he earned a Top 20 single with "Taxi" in 1972. Two years later "Cat's in the Cradle" was a #1. It was based on a poem by his wife, and told the story of a neglectful father too busy to pay attention to his son. It was poignant, affecting stuff, and Chapin delivered it with a haunting sense of compassion and loss. The song is still heard daily on radios across America.

Chapin wrote a musical, "The Night That Made America Famous," that received two Tony nominations in 1975; later that year the driven Chapin put out another album. The man was a legendarily hard worker, and his founding of WHY—World Hunger Year—in 1975 added another massive commitment to his agenda. In the next few years he would be a dynamo of charity work. He played an estimated two hundred concerts a year, and as many as half of them were charitable benefits. Chapin intensified his work on behalf of humanity in the moment of his greatest fame, taking full advantage of the bankability of his name to aid countless others he would never meet. He received numerous awards and honors, and in 1978 went to the White House to brief President Jimmy Carter on the need for activism against hunger.

In 1981 Chapin was to kick off a summer tour with a benefit at the Lakeside Theater in Eisenhower Park, Long Island. As he was driving himself to the gig, his car was struck from behind on the Long Island Expressway. His vehicle's gas tank ruptured, and the car exploded. An autopsy revealed that Chapin had a heart attack at some point before or during the accident.

In 1987 Chapin was honored with an all-star salute in Carnegie Hall; his widow, Sandy, was given the Special Congressional Gold Medal in his memory. It is estimated that Harry Chapin personally generated more than five million dollars during his charitable crusades.

Harry Chapin died too young, but in his way he was not a casualty of rock. During the years of his greatest success he avoided all the pitfalls and vices that litter rock 'n' roll history. Instead, he used his fame as a platform for helping others, with a supremely driven selflessness that has earned him an indelible mark in American culture. He accomplished more in his thirty-eight years than many of us could had we been afforded several lifetimes. Although much of his music has not aged as well, Chapin's example of altruism is one of rock's unique legacies. Multitalented Harry Chapin's life encompassed filmmaking, composing a musical, and making a permanent mark on the seventies singer-songwriter genre with his classic hit "Cat's in the Cradle." The most admirable aspect of his legacy was his sideline occupation of tireless activism on behalf of efforts to erase global hunger. Looking back on his labors, one imagines that Harry Chapin had a very big heart indeed. The world lost this crusading troubadour in a gruesome car accident on the Long Island Expressway, though his memory survives as an example of how stardom can be utilized rather than squandered.

A New Yorker and the son of a jazz drummer, Chapin sang in the Brooklyn Heights Boys Choir and spent time in the Air Force Academy and at Cornell University. In the sixties he started

Gene Clark

 ESSENTIAL LISTENING
The Byrds: *Greatest Hits*
Mr. Tambourine Man
Solo: *Echoes* (compilation)

ROCK AND ROLL HALL OF FAME
The Byrds inducted 1991

"Here Without You"

The Byrds enjoyed a couple years of dominance in the mid-sixties before fragmenting into a series of shifting lineups and finally imploding altogether. Central to the band's glory days, along with Roger McGuinn, David Crosby, and Chris Hillman, was singer-songwriter Gene Clark.

Clark was a handsome, rustic type from Tipton, Missouri, and was playing in the ultra-mainstream folk group the New Christy Minstrels when he met Crosby, He joined up with the newly formed Byrds, and was on board when "Mr. Tambourine Man" became a #1 single. Clark possessed one of the best voices in the Byrds' harmonic mix, and contributed "I'll Feel a Whole Lot Better," "Here Without You," and elements of "Eight Miles High" to the band's cover-heavy catalogue. Many were surprised when he left the band in 1966; but it was the first of several defections that would leave McGuinn the group's only original remaining member two years later.

One reason given for Clark's departure was that he was afraid of flying. While this was true, he also suffered from other phobias as well, including stage fright. Clark also had problems getting along with the rest of the group, McGuinn in particular. He would reportedly later say he had never intended to leave the Byrds on a permanent basis, but other than a one-off 1975 reunion album, he would never play in a legitimate form of the Byrds again. A patchy solo career followed, including 1971's White Light and 1974's No Other. Though he produced quality material, Clark lacked the name recognition and the ambition to match his success with the Byrds. He was a talented musician who apparently couldn't deal with the touring and promotion necessary for major rock success; instead of subjecting himself to trials he couldn't bear, he receded gradually into semiobscurity.

The Byrds's story was never an easy one to keep track of, what with myriad personnel changes over the years, brief re-formations and breakups, band members named Clark, Clarke, Gene Parsons, and Gram Parsons. In 1979, Gene Clark reunited with the two former main Byrds to form McGuinn, Clark & Hillman and released a Top 40 LP. Residual good feeling from this union had evaporated by 1987, when Clark joined with former Byrds drummer Michael Clarke to tour under the Byrds name; Clark and Clarke were sued by Crosby, McGuinn, and Hillman. Two years later the latter camp played a few shows together to establish a legal right to the Byrds name.

That Clark was reduced to hitting the road with an essentially phony version of a band he had departed more than twenty years earlier is an unfortunate illustration of how depressed his career had become. Years of heavy drinking finally brought down Gene Clark on May 24, 1991. Michael Clarke would continue touring with Michael Clarke's Byrds until his own death from liver failure in 1993.

43

Steve Clark
"Wasted"

ESSENTIAL LISTENING
Def Leppard: *Pyromania*

Def Leppard hit upon a blend of pop and metal in the eighties that earned them a remarkable string of hit LPs and singles, stadium-filling tours, and a license to excess that they made good use of and renewed with dutiful regularity. Along the way they earned the inevitable battle scars, the worst of which was the loss of founding guitarist Steve Clark to alcoholism.

With their elder members barely out of their teens, Def Leppard emerged in 1980 with a hit LP and began touring with the biggest names in heavy rock. They were young and photogenic, with a knack for catchy tunes combined with the requisite metal riffage. Their 1983 release, *Pyromania*, sold ten million copies; the follow-up, *Hysteria*, spawned six Top 20 singles in 1987. Def Leppard could do no wrong, and unlike many of their contemporaries managed to release relevant popular music well into the nineties.

The band suffered its first major setback in early 1985, when drummer Rick Allen lost an arm after suffering complications from an auto accident. Improbably, the group rallied around Allen and waited while he mastered a custom-designed drum kit. A similar sense of loyalty was extended at the time to guitarist Steve Clark, who was beginning a slide into chronic and debilitating alcoholism. Leppard was not an abstemious group by any means, but the growing scale of Clark's drinking began to adversely affect his health and his capacity for work. By the time of *Hysteria*, coguitarist Phil Collen was playing most parts in the studio. In 1989 Clark was found near comatose in a gutter after a drinking binge and was admitted to a psychiatric hospital.

While the rest of Def Leppard maintained at least a rock 'n' roll standard of sanity, Steve Clark was simply unable to win his fight with the bottle. The band fretted over his worsening condition until the end came on January 8, 1991. Clark was found dead in his London flat by his girlfriend after another drinking binge. The pathologist ruled that Clark had died after brain-stem compression caused by alcohol mixed with painkillers and antidepressant medication. The next year Def Leppard released a record that topped U.S. and U.K. charts.

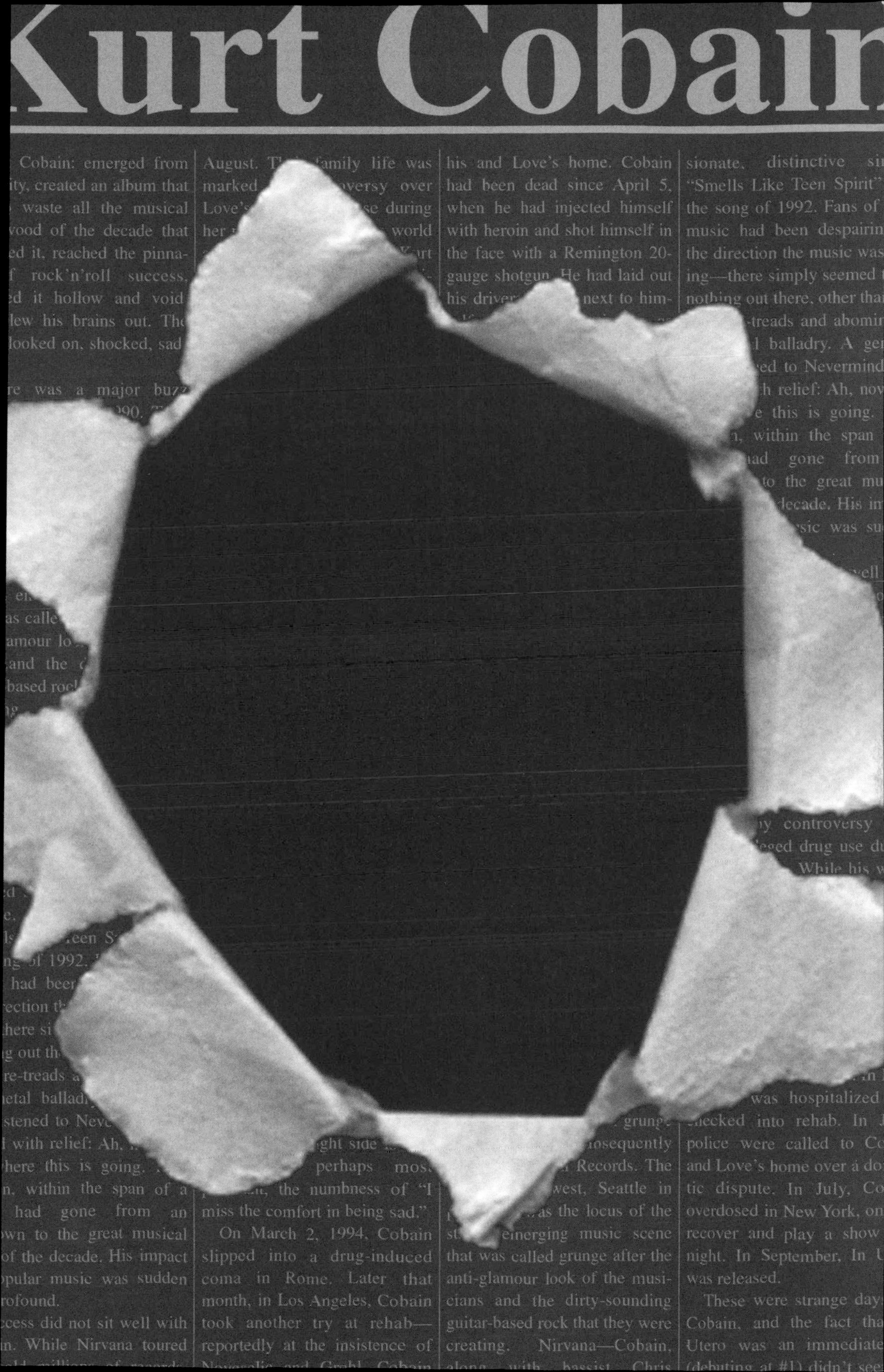

Cobain: emerged from
ity, created an album that
waste all the musical
wood of the decade that
ed it, reached the pinna-
f rock'n'roll success,
ed it hollow and void
lew his brains out. The
looked on, shocked, sad

re was a major buzz
990.

el
as calle
amour lo
and the
based roc
g

d
e.
Is een S
ng of 1992.
had been
rection th
here si
g out th
re-treads a
etal ballad
stened to Nev
i with relief: Ah,
here this is going.
n, within the span of a
had gone from an
wn to the great musical
of the decade. His impact
pular music was sudden
rofound.
ccess did not sit well with
n. While Nirvana toured

August. The family life was
marked oversy over
Love's se during
her world
Kurt
right side
perhaps mos
n, the numbness of "I
miss the comfort in being sad."

On March 2, 1994, Cobain
slipped into a drug-induced
coma in Rome. Later that
month, in Los Angeles, Cobain
took another try at rehab—
reportedly at the insistence of

his and Love's home. Cobain
had been dead since April 5,
when he had injected himself
with heroin and shot himself in
the face with a Remington 20-
gauge shotgun. He had laid out
his driver next to him-

grunge
nsequently
Records. The
west, Seattle in
as the locus of the
st emerging music scene
that was called grunge after the
anti-glamour look of the musicians and the dirty-sounding
guitar-based rock that they were
creating. Nirvana—Cobain,
along with bassist Chris

sionate, distinctive si
"Smells Like Teen Spirit"
the song of 1992. Fans of
music had been despairin
the direction the music was
ing—there simply seemed
nothing out there, other tha
-treads and abomin
l balladry. A ge
ed to Nevermind
h relief: Ah, nov
e this is going.
n, within the span
had gone from
to the great mu
decade. His i
sic was su

well

y controversy
leged drug use d
While his v

was hospitalized
hecked into rehab. In
police were called to Co
and Love's home over a do
tic dispute. In July, Co
overdosed in New York, on
recover and play a show
night. In September, In U
was released.

These were strange day
Cobain, and the fact tha
Utero was an immediate
(debuting at #1) didn't se

Kurt Cobain: emerged from obscurity, created an album that laid to waste all the musical deadwood of the decade that preceded it, reached the pinnacle of rock 'n' roll success, declared it hollow and void, then blew his brains out. The world looked on, shocked, saddened.

There was a major buzz around Nirvana in 1990. They had released their debut LP, *Bleach,* on Sub Pop—the independent label that was home to an army of grunge acts—and were subsequently signed to Geffen Records. The Pacific Northwest, Seattle in particular, was the locus of the strong emerging music scene that was called grunge after the antiglamour look of the musicians and the dirty-sounding guitar-based rock that they were creating. Nirvana— Cobain, along with bassist Krist Novoselic and drummer Dave Grohl—were to take their place at the head of the class.

"My Heart Is Broke"

))) **ESSENTIAL LISTENING**
Nevermind
In Utero

Nevermind, released in 1991, hit #1 and made a star of Kurt Cobain. He was an immensely talented songwriter and a passionate, distinctive singer. "Smells Like Teen Spirit" was *the* song of 1992. Fans of rock music had been despairing of the direction pop music was taking—there simply seemed to be nothing out there, other than the usual retreads and abominable soft-metal balladry. A generation listened to *Nevermind* and sighed with relief: *Ah, now we see where this is going.* Kurt Cobain, within the span of a year, had gone from an unknown to the great musical hope of the decade. His impact on popular music was sudden and profound.

Success did not sit well with Cobain. While Nirvana toured and sold millions of records, Cobain expressed his inner emptiness. In interviews he mocked his own success and complained of mysterious stomach pains. He married Courtney Love in February 1992, and the couple produced a daughter in August. Their family life was marked by controversy over Love's alleged drug use during her pregnancy. While his world swirled and churned, Kurt Cobain set about the grim business of developing a heroin addiction that would haunt him until his death.

In 1993, the cloud of trouble around Cobain darkened. Nirvana began recording a new album early in the year. In May, Cobain was hospitalized and checked into rehab. In June, police were called to Cobain and Love's home over a domestic dispute. In July, Cobain overdosed in New York, only to recover and play a show that night. In September, *In Utero* was released.

These were strange days for Cobain, and the fact that *In Utero* was an immediate hit (debuting at #1) didn't seem to offer him much solace. His song titles speak volumes: "All Apologies," "Rape Me." For *The Beavis and Butt-Head Experience* LP, Cobain contributed a cheerful track called "I Hate Myself and Want to Die." Cobain's nihilism and black mind-set were out on public display, and music lovers were confronted with a brilliant performer bent on inflicting his inner pain on his audience. The lyric sheet for *In Utero* reads, in retrospect, like a suicide note, with lines such as "throw me in the fire," "my heart is broke," "look on the bright side is suicide," and, perhaps most poignant, the numbness of "I miss the comfort in being sad."

On March 2, 1994, Cobain slipped into a drug-induced coma in Rome. Later that month, in Los Angeles, Cobain took another try at rehab—reportedly at the insistence of Novoselic and Grohl. Cobain soon escaped the rehab center and disappeared. On April 4, his mother filed a missing-persons report. On April 8, an electrician contracted to install a burglar alarm found Cobain's body in the garage apartment adjacent to his and Love's home. Cobain had been dead since April 5, when he had injected himself with heroin and shot himself in the face with a Remington 20-gauge shotgun. He had laid out his driver's license next to himself before his suicide, as though to say: *Here, this is me. Make no mistake about what happened here.*

British writer G. K. Chesterton wrote that suicide is more violent than murder because the murderer takes one life, while the suicide kills everyone and effectively destroys the world. Kurt Cobain had extraordinary talent, wealth, and fame, and he wanted nothing to do with it. His mental anguish and drug addiction could not be assuaged by notoriety, success, and money. Kurt Cobain entertained us with his gift for a couple of years, and then he blotted out the sun. He simply didn't want to be here with us.

1938–1960

Eddie Cochran

ESSENTIAL LISTENING
*Somethin' Else: The Fine Lookin'
Hits of Eddie Cochran*

ROCK AND ROLL HALL OF FAME
Inducted 1987

Mr. Versatility

Eddie Cochran was an early devotee of the recording studio technology that enabled multitracking and overdubbing. On his singles "Summertime Blues" and "C'mon Everybody" he played and sang every part that eventually appeared on record.

At the Scene of the Crash

"At one point I woke up in the ambulance, and I was holding [Cochran's] hand, and I thought he'd regain consciousness, but he never did. The ambulance attendant told me later he knew we were in love, and so he'd locked our hands in case we came to."

—Sharon Sheeley,
Eddie Cochran's fiancée

"Three Steps to Heaven"

Southern California's Eddie Cochran was a pioneer of rock's early days who penned one of its most immortal tunes, then died an untimely death in a car accident while still in his early twenties.

Cochran started playing country music as a teenager and recorded as one-half of the Cochran Brothers in 1955 (confusingly, Eddie and Hank Cochran were not related). The next year Elvis Presley introduced rock 'n' roll to the world, and Cochran was appropriately inspired. He met young songwriter Jerry Capeheart while buying guitar strings, and the two struck up a partnership. Cochran got a big break in 1956, when he sang "Twenty Flight Rock" in the film *The Girl Can't Help It*. Cochran, young and charismatic, was hired to appear in another film later in the year. In 1957 he scored a Top 20 hit with "Sittin' in the Balcony." The next year he cemented his place in history with the release of "Summertime Blues," which was a Top 10 single and remains one of rock's primal classics.

Apparently suffering from fear of flying after the plane crash that killed Buddy Holly, Ritchie Valens, and the Big Bopper, Cochran recorded a tribute ("Three Steps to Heaven") to the three fallen rockers and subsequently avoided airplanes as much as his steady touring schedule would permit. While his recordings by decade's end failed to match the lofty chart standards of "Summertime Blues," Cochran was a big star in Britain, and he toured there to capitalize. On April 17, 1960, Cochran had just finished a tour and hired a taxi bound for London, where he was bound to catch a transatlantic flight back home to the U.S. The car skidded into a roadside lamppost; although the driver and tour manager in the front seat weren't injured, the passengers in the back of the car fared far worse. Gene Vincent—another early rocker who had coheadlined the tour—suffered a broken collarbone and ribs. Cochran's fiancée, Sharon Sheeley (a successful rock songwriter) incurred a broken pelvis. Eddie Cochran was catapulted headfirst through the windshield. He was taken to the hospital right away but survived his brain injuries less than a day. Cochran's body was returned to the U.S. and buried in southern California.

1935–1964

Sam COOKE

An Endorsement from the Greatest
In 1964, after defeating Sonny Liston in a heavyweight championship fight in Miami Beach, Cassius Clay (later Muhammad Ali) pronounced his opinion that "Sam Cooke is the world's greatest rock 'n' roll singer— the greatest singer in the world." Cook returned the good word by inviting Clay for a televised duet.

"Wonderful World"

Chicagoan Sam Cooke's sophisticated, crystalline singing voice and dapper image launched him from the world of gospel music to secular pop and R&B. His voice and image would heavily influence the next wave of soul singers such as Al Green, but by then he would be gone, his unblemished image compromised after he was shot to death in a shady L.A. motel.

Cooke was the son of a minister and grew up singing in the church. By the time he was twenty, he was singing lead for the Soul Stirrers—a plum position with one of the top American gospel groups. Cooke spent more than five years at the microphone for the Soul Stirrers, but his gospel-singing soul was apparently also stirred by a strong ambition for pop success. He recorded a secular song under the name "Dale Cooke" to throw the gospel crowd off the track. A more imaginative cover name might have worked more effectively; Cooke's ruse was quickly detected, and Sam Cooke became a solo artist.

It seemed that Cooke had made the right decision. He possessed strong songwriting skills to augment his vocal command, and he enjoyed a string of hits beginning in 1957 with the #1 "You Send Me"—written by Cooke but credited to his brother due to contractual hassles. After a move to RCA Records, Cooke began a run as a Top 40 national artist. His procession of hits, many self-penned, included such incontestable classics as "Chain Gang," "Twistin' the Night Away," "Another Saturday Night," and the enduring "Wonderful World." Cooke was able to fuse elements of blues and gospel—instrumental crunch combined with impassioned vocals—with an open, clear production sound that hit commercial paydirt. Cooke was also lining his nest with smart business moves, branching out into production, music publishing, and establishing his own record label.

Cooke's best-laid plans went awry, though, when he was murdered in Los Angeles on December 11, 1964. He was staying at the three-dollar-a-night Hacienda Motel with a twenty-two-year-old girl after an evening of nightclubbing. Details are murky, but motel manager Bertha Franklin reported that she shot Cooke after he attempted to rape the young girl, then turned on Franklin herself when his intended victim tried to contact the police. After an investigation the coroner's office ruled that it was a case of justifiable homicide. For some, the circumstances of Sam Cooke's murder were never adequately explained. A week after his death, he was buried in Chicago. Two hundred thousand fans reportedly attended, and performers at the service included Bobby "Blue" Bland, Ray Charles, and Lou Rawls.

ESSENTIAL LISTENING
Solo: *Greatest Hits*
With the Soul Stirrers: *Sam Cooke with the Soul Stirrers*

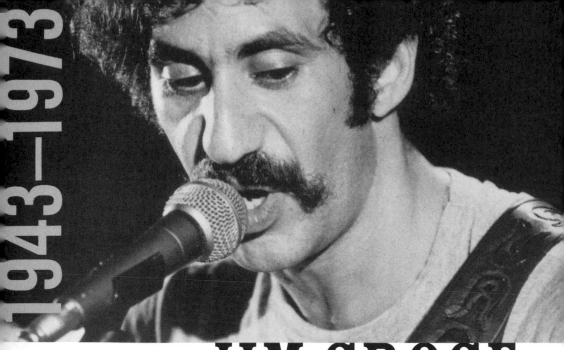

JIM CROCE
"You Don't Mess Around with Jim"

Jim Croce's folk-tinged songwriting toyed with a tongue-in-cheek badass persona and sensitive-guy paeans to enduring love. He was a distinctive stylist who was chasing his new-found fame hard when he died at thirty in a plane crash in Louisiana.

When success found him, Philadelphia native Jim Croce responded by working hard and hitting the road. Perhaps years of assorted and sundry prefame occupations girded him for a sweat-of-the-brow approach. While honing his craft, Croce at various times toiled as a toy-store clerk, truck driver, telephone lineman, summer-camp teacher, and construction worker. The latter job left the most lasting impression on Croce when he smashed a finger with a sledge-hammer and subsequently had to reconfigure his guitar-playing style.

After a misfire LP recorded with his wife in 1969, Croce sent some of his songs to music producer and college friend Tommy West. Impressed, West invited Croce into the studio. The result was the 1972 LP *You Don't Mess Around with Jim*. The title track was a Top 10 hit that year, and "Operator" from the same album

hit the Top 20. The next year Croce topped the charts with "Bad, Bad Leroy Brown," a semi-comedic narrative of a scary street hustler. Croce was carving out a niche for himself as a world-wise songsmith with a heart of gold. It was a winning image, and his acoustic-based tunes fit perfectly with the times.

Later in 1973 Croce's story came to an abrupt end when he finished a concert at Northwestern State University of Louisiana on September 20 and boarded a plane to perform his second show of the day, in Sherman, Texas. His chartered Beechcraft D-18 twin-engine airplane hit a tree during takeoff. Croce died with five others in the crash, including his guitarist Maury Muehleisen. The LP Croce had been working on at the time of his death, *I Got a Name*, was released two months later and was a hit—the title track placed in the Top 10, and "Time in a Bottle" was a #1. Jim Croce's tragic end arrived when he was at the top of the charts, the apex of his craft, and perfectly in step with the moment.

ESSENTIAL LISTENING
Photographs and Memories
Time in a Bottle

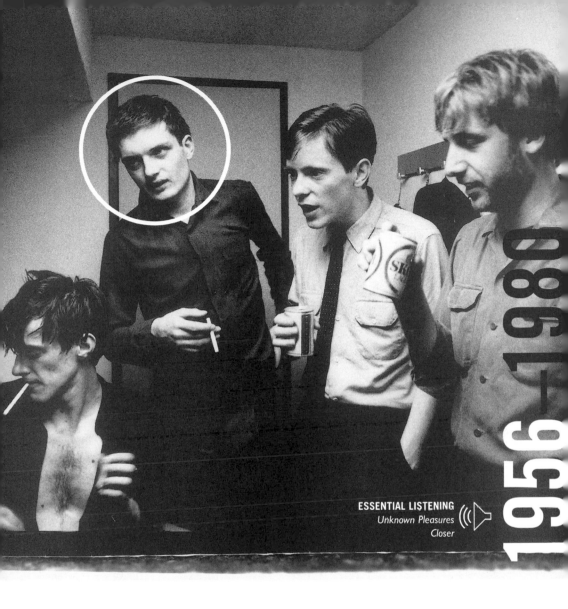

ESSENTIAL LISTENING
Unknown Pleasures
Closer

1956–1980

Ian Curtis

"Love Will Tear Us Apart"

Joy Division may have become a footnote to the success story of New Order, the band that rose from its ashes, but in hindsight the group was a vital missing link between Bowie's seventies and Nirvana's nineties. They were gloom merchants of the highest rank, and at the center of their bleak vision was singer Ian Curtis, whose short brush with success and fame would end with his suicide.

Joy Division—named after the organized prostitution camp that served the Nazi military—formed after various band members were energized by a Sex Pistols performance in Manchester, England, in 1976. Guitarist Bernard Sumner, bassist Peter Hook, and drummer Stephen Morris were joined by Ian Curtis after the latter responded to an ad posted at a local record store. By 1978 their performances had generated sufficient buzz to generate offers of record deals. Of no little interest to audiences was Curtis's performing style; the singer onstage was invariably described as a "man possessed."

Their first LP, *Unknown Pleasures,* was a work of staggering bleakness and sporadic beauty. The music was sparse, pulsing, and heavy, and Curtis's vocals and lyrics explored a terrain of romantic alienation that spoke to every teenager—or, indeed, to anyone who had ever been a teenager. In 1979, the year of the LP's release, the group would tour the U.K. and pick up a national reputation as a group to be watched in the future. Curtis's dark stance was no pose, though, and in the first flush of success his life and psyche would decline alarmingly.

Early that year, Curtis was diagnosed with epilepsy after suffering grand mal seizures. He lived in constant fear of these attacks, which could strike him onstage if he was exposed to strobe lights. Although he had enjoyed the first bloom of Joy Division's accomplishments, his affliction with epilepsy reportedly worsened his propensity for depression and dark moods. His state of mind was further strained that year when he began an extramarital affair.

In March of 1980, Joy Division recorded their second LP in London. Two months later Curtis was in the hospital after ingesting an overdose of drugs. He took a few weeks off while Joy Division planned an American tour to capitalize on the strength of their new album. Two days before the projected breakthrough tour, Ian Curtis talked his wife into spending the night at her parents' house, then whiled away an evening alone listening to music (Iggy Pop's *The Idiot*), watching a film (Werner Herzog's *Stroszek*), and composing his suicide note. The letter was addressed to his wife, and at the end he noted that the sun was rising and that he was listening to the sound of morning birds singing. He then put his neck in a noose and hung himself. Weeks later, the song "Love Will Tear Us Apart" was a Top 20 success in the U.K. In 1995 Curtis's widow would release *Touching from a Distance,* a revealing biography of Curtis that detailed his mental instability and eccentricities.

Rather than pack it in after losing their front man, the surviving members of Joy Division regrouped as New Order, emphasized synthesizers and a driving beat, and improbably became a pop sensation in the mid-eighties. Ian Curtis's name has lived on as an icon of the romantic extremes of adolescent pain, a legacy not entirely at odds with the details of his short life. He was also instrumental in the creation of two Joy Division albums that married a highly original instrumental approach with harrowing vocals that still sound remarkably fresh today.

Buddy Holly
Ritchie Valens
The Big Bopper

"The Day the Music Died"

These three young men, by a cruel stroke of fate, have been linked in rock 'n' roll history since they died together in a small-plane crash outside Clear Lake, Iowa, in 1959. They were three of the biggest rock stars of their time, and the impact of their death remains difficult to comprehend after the passage of more than forty years. Their tragic demise represented a loss of innocence for a generation of teenagers; some contend the plane crash instigated America's painful process of disillusionment in the sixties, sparked by John Kennedy's assassination and the ethical ambiguities of Vietnam. Whatever the case, no one could deny that rock music lost three of its originators on a cold, snowy midwestern night in 1959.

Buddy Holly was from Lubbock, Texas, and grew up in a home teeming with music. He showed natural talent early, and by his teens he had formed a band and was playing on local radio. He was about twenty when Elvis Presley made it big, and from that moment Holly knew what he wanted to do. After a false start in Nashville, Holly named his backing group the Crickets and drove to producer Norman Petty's New Mexico studio to cut a record. The result—"That'll Be the Day"—was a #1 in 1957.

ROCK AND ROLL HALL OF FAME
Inducted 1986

Buddy Holly

1936–1959

Holly was driven and ambitious, and he compressed a life's work into his two-year recording career. By the end of 1958 he had added an exhilarating series of classic hits to his resume: "Peggy Sue," "Oh, Boy!," "Rave On," "Everyday," "Not Fade Away," and "It's So Easy." He was an unlikely rock star, with his bespectacled countenance and gangly frame, but he made the most of a fallow period in which Elvis was in the army, Jerry Lee Lewis had fallen to scandal, and Little Richard had temporarily abandoned rock 'n' roll for the embrace of the church. In late 1958 Holly left the Crickets and entered into a legal dispute with his producer; as a result, he was cash-poor and forced to take part in a cold-weather tour of frozen midwestern towns called the Winter Dance Party.

If Holly's recording career was brief, Ritchie Valens's lasted but a heartbeat. Born Richard Valenzuela in Pacoima, California, Valens was raised in poverty but obtained a guitar and learned to play at an early age. He was a stocky powerhouse of a performer, and after time spent in local bands he signed with an L.A. label and focused on his songwriting. In 1958 he had a regional smash with "Come On, Let's Go," then the next year hit #2 with the double-sided single "Donna"/"La Bamba." The former was a ballad written for his girlfriend who lived on the other side of the tracks. The latter was based on a traditional Mexican song, and its infectious three-chord stomp cemented Valens's status as

an overnight success story. When he was booked on the Winter Dance Party, his star was definitely in ascendance.

The Big Bopper was, at the time, arguably the most popular act on the tour. He was riding a wave of international success with the hit single "Chantilly Lace." The Bopper was the alter ego of J. P. Richardson, a DJ from Beaumont, Texas. He was a family man determined to make a better life for his wife and children, and worked numerous daily on-air shifts. His most popular creation was the Big Bopper: a hyper, jiving maniac whose proto-raps were laced with hipster slang and innuendo. The Bopper was such a convincing character that many listeners assumed he was African American and never connected him to J. P. Richardson. Richardson was also a songwriter in his spare time, and in the exploding rock-music business he saw a means to express his talent and earn extra money. In 1958 he recorded a novelty tune called "The Purple People Eater Meets the Witch-Doctor." The public yawned with apathy until DJs began playing the largely improvised flip side, "Chantilly Lace." Suddenly the Big Bopper was a major hit, and Richardson—a big man with a profound sense of fun—cooked up a stage act and hit the road with the Winter Dance Party.

The Winter Dance Party was, by unanimous accounts, a fiasco. Although the shows were energized and exciting, the conditions the musicians endured were nothing short of awful. It was January in the upper Midwest, and the tour moved along snow-swept highways in ramshackle school buses. Poor scheduling forced the tour to traverse hundreds of miles daily. Breakdowns and heating failures were commonplace, and the players reached a breaking point midway through the grueling itinerary. Valens was a teenager from southern California who'd never dealt with cold weather or been away from home for very long. The Bopper was suffering from the flu and had trouble fitting his outsized frame into the cramped sleeping quarters on the bus. Holly, the most seasoned star on the tour, was accustomed to traveling with at least a modicum of comfort. He seethed with indignity and counted the days until he could return to his new Greenwich Village apartment.

On February 3, 1959, the Winter Dance Party reached Clear Lake, Iowa. The weather was cold and blustery, and the tour bus arrived barely in time to play a show at the local Surf Ballroom. By this time a strong camaraderie had developed among the rockers, and they sat in on each other's sets in a series of spirited performances. The crowd, unaccustomed to seeing acts of such magnitude in their midst, responded with appropriate pent-up small-town teen fervor.

By show's end, Holly decided he could take no more. The next concert was scheduled in Moorehead, Minnesota, and the itinerary was so tight they would have to board the bus directly after leaving the stage. Dreaming of a warm bed, a hot meal, and time to clean his stage clothes, Holly asked the Surf Ballroom's manager to locate a plane to charter. Holly planned to bring along his backing band along in the four-seat craft, but after some backstage wrangling Valens and the Bopper arranged to take the two open seats.

The sky was clear when the Surf Ballroom show ended, but by the time they were ready to take off, snow was blowing across the plains. Twenty-one-year-old pilot Roger Peterson was reportedly hesitant about taking off in the worsening conditions, but after receiving clearance from the control tower, the three musicians joined him in the craft and they left the ground sometime after midnight.

Painful Memory
"There was a thing that happened that night. Buddy was leaning back against the wall in this cane-bottom chair laughing at me. He says, 'You're not going on the plane tonight, huh?' I said no. He said, 'Well, I hope your bus freezes up.' And I said, 'Well, I hope your plane crashes.' I was awful young, and it took me a long time to get over that."
—Waylon Jennings
(bass, the Crickets)

1941–1959

 ROCK AND ROLL HALL OF FAME
Inducted 2001

Ritchie Valens

The plane soon disappeared from radar and radio, and by morning the truth was learned: The flight had crashed shortly after takeoff. Rescuers located the plane on a farm field, and one look at the twisted wreckage precluded any hope of finding survivors. The pilot was wedged inside the shattered metal frame, and the three rockers had been thrown clear and died on impact. By mid-morning, news broke all around the world that three of the brightest American rock stars had perished together in this brutal accident.

Fans and family mourned the loss of the three young men—each of whom is invariably remembered as gracious, down-to-earth, and likable. Their talents were missed as well; rock plunged into a fallow period that would be reinvigorated only several years later with the breakthrough success of four Buddy Holly fans who called themselves the Beatles. The terrible impact of the Iowa plane crash was immortalized in 1972 with the release of Don McLean's #1 single "American Pie." The song memorialized Holly, Valens, and the Bopper, and recounted the jarring loss of innocence America's teens experienced upon learning of the plane crash that took their lives. Film tributes followed: *The Buddy Holly Story* in 1978 and *La Bamba* in 1987.

Holly, Valens, and the Big Bopper have been joined forever by the tragedy that took their lives. It bears remembering that, in their moment, they were vital, dynamic rock 'n' roll pioneers. Their existence was defined by energy and excitement, until a capricious turn of fate froze their legacy and linked them forever.

ESSENTIAL LISTENING
Buddy Holly: *Greatest Hits*
Ritchie Valens: *The Very Best of Ritchie Valens*
The Big Bopper: *Hellooo Baby!: Best of Big Bopper*

The Big Bopper
(J. P. Richardson)

1930–1959

Pete De Freitas

"Heaven Up Here"

The original lineup of Echo and the Bunnymen formed in Liverpool and featured singer Ian McCulloch backed by bass, guitar, and a drum machine named Echo. Despite the apparent job security implied by top billing, Echo was fired when the Bunnymen entered the studio to record their first album. Enter drummer Pete De Freitas.

De Freitas drummed on what is now considered the classic run of Bunnymen LPs: *Heaven Up Here, Porcupine,* and *Ocean Rain.* Bunnymen music, never nearly as popular in America as it was in the U.K., featured evocative atmospheric post–new wave rumblings fronted by McCulloch's quasi–Jim Morrison vocals. They were among the best of their early-eighties British rock class.

Though the Bunnymen weren't known as particularly hard-living—at least by musicians' standards—beginning on New Year's Eve 1985 De Freitas reportedly undertook an episode of vigorous debauchery that ranks among rock 'n' roll's all-time most colorful. On a quest to create a band they would call the Sex Gods, De Freitas and accomplices took large quantities of cocaine and strong hallucinogenics and found themselves in New Orleans. In line with their ego-shattering endeavor, the crew took on new identities—De Freitas became an omniscient being called Louie. Perhaps feeling he hadn't gone far enough, De Freitas then stayed awake for—one witness insists—eighteen days. De Freitas was also reportedly involved with the daughter of the local chief of police, which eventually necessitated a getaway to Jamaica.

What a hangover *that* must have been. De Freitas prudently took leave of the Bunnymen the next year, though he returned for a post-McCulloch version of the band. During rehearsals for that album, he was killed in a motorcycle accident in Liverpool. Though stories of his onetime excesses make for enjoyable retelling, in the end De Freitas was a young man who was tragically killed before reaching his thirtieth birthday.

 ESSENTIAL LISTENING
Porcupine
Songs to Learn and Sing (compilation)

SANDY DENNY

"No More Sad Refrains"

1947–1978

British singer-songwriter Sandy Denny has been called the English Janis Joplin for her propensity for excess, her wild heart, and her outsized talent. She was one of the best-known U.K. female performers of her time, largely due to her tenure with the venerable Fairport Convention, although her substance abuse exacerbated personal problems and led to a career decline. Her unfortunate death in 1978 came after a drunken fall at home and injuries whose severity she tragically misjudged.

Denny came out of the coffeehouse folk scene armed with a fine voice and songwriting talent; she joined Fairport Convention in 1968 and appeared prominently on the band's watershed *Liege and Lief*. After Fairport she went on to a solo career, forming Fotheringay, then stepped out under her own name. She toured and recorded successfully in the early seventies and was named best British female vocalist by *Melody Maker* in both 1970 and 1971. American rock fans might remember her best as the covocalist on Led Zeppelin's haunting Tolkienesque "The Battle of Evermore."

Another less-profitable stint with Fairport followed, then a swift personal decline brought on by alcohol and drugs. Denny had a daughter in 1977, but her cocaine and alcohol usage were so severe that she reportedly suffered withdrawal symptoms while in hospital following delivery. Postnatal depression and the strain of taking care of a small child overwhelmed Denny, and in early 1978 her husband left, taking their daughter. Soon after she fell down a flight of stairs in her house while intoxicated. She was cut and suffered headaches for more than a week, but failed to seek medical attention. On April 21, she was dead from head injuries she had sustained. A fine voice and gifted writer had been silenced by drugs, booze, and pressures too great for her to bear.

ESSENTIAL LISTENING
The Best of Sandy Denny
With Fairport Convention: *Liege and Lief*

"Take Me to Tomorrow"

J ohn Denver emerged in the seventies as one of America's most popular singer-songwriters; his gentle touch with ballads and his facility with love songs and paeans to nature ensconced him firmly as pop's preeminent exponent of all things mellow and back-to-nature. After a run of phenomenal success relatively hard times followed, with a dearth of chart success and a drinking problem that led to his arrest for driving under the influence. Finally fans were saddened to learn of Denver's death following a single-engine plane crash into the Pacific Ocean.

Born John Henry Deutschendorf in UFO hot spot Roswell, New Mexico, the singer was born into an air force family, his childhood spent in the American South and Japan followed by enrollment in Texas Tech's architecture program. He cut his musical teeth on a vintage Gibson guitar bestowed upon him by his grandmother, and by the mid-sixties he was working at the drafting table by day and playing folk clubs at night in Los Angeles. He received his first big break in 1965, when he beat out two hundred fifty other contenders to join the Chad Mitchell Trio (replacing, oddly, Chad Mitchell). The Trio were relatively big fish in the folky pond, and after naming himself after his favorite city John Denver went on to tour and record with the group.

Every Little Bit Helps

In 1988 *Aviation Week and Space Technology* reported that John Denver had approached the Soviets about launching him up to their *Mir* space station. Officials in the USSR were reported to think about it—for an asking price of ten million dollars. Although nothing came of the idea, in 1990 the band New Order reached a financial settlement with Denver's publisher over an alleged copyright infringement stemming from one of the group's songs. After paying the agreed amount, the band's Steven Morris said, "It's New Order's contribution to sending John Denver into space."

John Denver

ESSENTIAL LISTENING
John Denver's Greatest Hits

In 1969 Denver released the solo *Rhymes and Reasons*; while the LP caused little stir, it contained "Leaving on a Jet Plane," which was a #1 hit for Peter, Paul and Mary. Denver was well on his way, and by 1971 his "Take Me Home, Country Roads" hit #2; its parent LP went gold, and the next year's *Rocky Mountain High* LP became a Top 10 hit. These were the years after the mind-warping sixties, leading into the dual defeats of Watergate and Vietnam. America yearned for a voice of simplicity and songs of mellow beauty. Denver was there to fill the need, and he did so admirably. His best singles were yearning odes to transcendence and natural majesty that managed to avoid leaving a saccharine aftertaste.

The next few years belonged to John Denver. A greatest hits compilation released in 1974 stayed on the charts for two years and sold ten million copies. He scored #1s with "Sunshine on My Shoulders," "Annie's Song" (written for his wife), "Thank God I'm a Country Boy," and "I'm Sorry." His albums routinely topped the charts well into the mid-seventies, and placed in the Top 10 for a few years afterward. In 1977 Denver stretched out into film with the George Burns comedy *Oh, God!* and in 1980 he starred in a Muppets Christmas special on national TV. With his unassuming sheepdog look and the undeniably consistent quality of his work, Denver saw out the seventies as one of the most famed pop artists of the decade.

Then, inevitably, things changed. Early-eighties LPs grazed the Top 40, but soon Denver found himself one of many artists rendered obsolete and anachronistic in the pastel glow of MTV. By 1985, his album *Dreamland Express* barely caused a ripple in the Top 100. Denver chose not to go quietly. He focused on his political convictions, touring the Soviet Union, playing benefits, and doing volunteer work against nuclear power and for environmental causes.

The heal-the-planet underpinnings of his artistic vision began to flower in concerts such as his 1987 concert in the USSR to benefit victims of Chernobyl. The year before, he had been dropped from his record company amid speculation that its corporate owner—big-time arms contractor General Electric—was none too pleased with his tune "Let Us Begin (What Are We Making Weapons For?)."

In the nineties Denver continued to tour and play benefits for left-wing causes. His few releases sold mainly to diehards, although he continued to maintain a respectable presence on the road and succeeded in bringing mainly ecological issues to the attention of his audience. But it was during these years that depression and alcohol abuse began to factor into his life; his second marriage failed and he was charged in 1993 and 1994 in separate drunk-driving incidents.

On October 12, 1997, Denver played eighteen holes of golf in Pebble Beach, then later in the day took off from Monterey Peninsula Airport in his single-engine Long-EZ—an experimental plane that he had just purchased. The aircraft plunged into Monterey Bay approximately one hundred yards from shore at approximately 5:30 in the afternoon. Denver was killed in the accident. The National Transportation Safety Board stated two days later that Denver—a longtime aviation enthusiast—had been flying illegally because of his impaired-driving arrests. Although there was speculation that Denver's crash was a suicide, no substantial evidence has ever backed the claim.

John Denver experienced soaring highs of fame to match the splendor he evoked in his song lyrics. His untimely death caps the legacy of an artist who, long after the finger of fame had pointed elsewhere, continued to ply his craft and pursue his convictions.

Nicholas "Razzle" Dingley

"All the Wasted Years"

As drummer for mid-eighties metal band Hanoi Rocks, "Razzle" Dingley abused the skins with appropriate vigor and thrash. What he would unfortunately be most remembered for, however, was dying in Mötley Crüe singer Vince Neil's car.

"Razzle" Dingley was born on December 2nd on the Isle of Wight, just off the center of southern England. Influenced by such bands as The Sex Pistols and The Damned, "Razzle" Dingley took up the drums in 1977. Early on he played in the band Fuck Pigs, Demon Preachers, and The Dark. In 1982, after seeing a performance at the Zigzag club in London, Razzle joined Hanoi Rocks, replacing drummer Gyp Casino. The Finnish "sleaze rock" band, founded in 1980 by singer Michael Monroe and guitarist Andy McCoy, was largely influenced by 70's glam rock, specifically David Bowie and The New York Dolls. Razzle instantly seemed to assimilate with band members and by the end of 1983 Hanoi Rocks went on tour in the U.S.

On December 8, 1984, Neil and assorted bandmates and scene makers were involved in a bout of heavy partying when Neil decided to head out for supplies—undeterred by the nagging reality of his immense intoxication. Dingley came along for the ride, and Neil crashed his 1972 Ford Pantera sports car in Redondo Beach; Dingley was killed in the accident, and two passengers in another car were seriously injured. Dingley's death as passenger in a drunk-driving accident became one of too many such tragic and deeply stupid incidents.

Neil, to atone for his actions, served twenty days in jail accompanied by an arduous two hundred hours of community service and the onerous burden of lecturing on the evils of booze and drugs. He also paid out two million six hundred thousand dollars in compensation to the people he had injured.

ESSENTIAL LISTENING
Two Steps from the Move

1948–1974

Nick Drake

"Safe in the Womb of an Everlasting Night"

Success eluded him. Depression gnawed at his mind. His songs were steeped in melancholia. In the decades since his death, Nick Drake has been remembered by a cult audience as a quintessential tortured poet, his wistful voice and languorous, introspective songs presaging his early death from an overdose following a period of semiretirement from the music business. Drake would finally reach the mass audience that had dodged him during his life a full quarter century after his passing, when one of his songs was used in a 1999 Volkswagen TV commercial. Hearing Drake's haunted voice, millions asked the identity of the ad's mystery singer. They unfortunately learned that Nick Drake left this world decades ago.

Drake grew up in an affluent English hamlet, and a pastoral meditative quality would typify his music. He was discovered while still a student at Cambridge University in 1968, and the next year recorded *Five Leaves Left* for Island Records. The record was not a pop success, but those who discovered it enthusiastically absorbed Drake's complex finger-picking acoustic guitar, otherworldly voice, and densely poetic lyrics. Drake was a visionary troubadour of sorts, but he was constitutionally unable to tackle the demands of the press and the public—he was introverted and pained onstage, and had few dealings with interviewers or his audience.

In 1970 Drake released *Bryter Layter*, another rich-textured effort that enjoyed little commercial success. Drake's music was meditative and wistful, with an undertow of desperation that belied its surface beauty. He sang cryptically about his distaste for the traps and attachments of the world, and seemed at times to be writing mainly about the internal workings of his own mind. Withdrawal from reality was a prominent feature of his own existence by this time, and in 1970 he abdicated any hope of future live performances. His shyness and melancholia had developed into full-blown mental illness, a depression of such magnitude that he reportedly neglected his hygiene and spent days alone and catatonic.

Drake became a recluse, recording 1972's *Pink Moon* alone with only voice and guitar. One account has him sending the tapes to his record label via mail, another claims he dropped them at the company's reception desk and disappeared before he could be recognized.

Drake was dogged by his continued inability to find an audience. His songs were his best—perhaps his only—chance of connecting with the outside world. Some who knew him indicate that he was on a personal mission to somehow break out of the cage of his illness and communicate his singular reality to the rest of humanity. When his records were largely ignored, he despaired about ever having voiced his thoughts. He entered a psychiatric hospital and vowed never to wrote songs again. When he was released, he was taking antidepressant medication and obtained a job as a computer programmer. By 1974 he had recovered enough to begin writing again. Drake recorded four new songs, but on November 25, he was found dead in his parents' home. He had overdosed on his antidepressant medication.

A coroner's report indicated that Drake had probably committed suicide, while friends and family have staunchly denied that was the case. Whatever the circumstances of his demise, Nick Drake has inarguably become more successful in death than in life. His work has been repeatedly repackaged and rereleased as word of his strangely poignant music has spread from one generation to the next. Drake's music went national in 1999 when a Volkswagen commercial used his song "Pink Moon." The ad itself was surprisingly evocative, and suited Drake's music with as much suitability as any literal image might be expected to. Record store clerks across the country were inundated with requests for the identity of "that guy who sings in the Volkswagen commercial." The answer: Nick Drake, an elusive artist who released a handful of beautiful and sometimes harrowing recordings before dying at twenty-six.

 ESSENTIAL LISTENING
Five Leaves Left, Bryter Later, Pink Moon—
Drake's three recordings form an indispensable body of work. First-timers might prefer the compilation *Way to Blue: An Introduction to Nick Drake.*

1973–1995

Eazy-E

ESSENTIAL LISTENING (((▷
With N.W.A.: *Straight Outta Compton*

"Straight Outta Compton"

N.W.A. pioneered the genre of gangsta rap, with their spot-on reporting of life in gang-infested South Central Los Angeles, their aggressive sound, and their vociferous disrespect for law enforcement. At the center of their unstable mix of characters was Eazy-E, the rapper who marshaled the initial incarnation of the group together and presided over its latter days following the defection of key members. His death from AIDS came as a shock to everyone—including Eazy-E himself, who apparently didn't suspect he had the illness until a month before his death.

Eazy-E was born Eric Wright in L.A. While some other members of N.W.A. (short for "Niggaz with Attitude," an in-your-face moniker that shocked the uninitiated) came from stable middle-class backgrounds, Eazy had lived the lifestyle his group would rap about. A former drug dealer, he invested his profits in founding Ruthless Records and set about trying to break into rap music. He enlisted friends including O'Shea Jackson and Andre Young—better known as Ice Cube and Dr. Dre, respectively—and began forging a brutal new sound that reflected the chaos and danger of life for young African Americans living amid gang wars and drive-by shootings.

In 1989, N.W.A. found the right combination and released a classic. *Straight Outta Compton* was a major hit and a groundbreaking moment in popular music. Uncompromising and profane, it crystallized young African-American male rage and sold it to an audience of millions. The LP contained an extremely pissed-off tune called "Fuck tha Police" that was nothing less than an open attack on law enforcement in artistic retaliation for decades of perceived repression and brutality. The track focused media attention on the group and earned a none-too-subtle letter of warning from the FBI.

The group was a focal point for controversy, and their revolutionary rage gave them an aura of real menace. N.W.A. didn't start a dialogue about American race relations; instead they unleashed a sonic storm of anger and defied anyone to silence them. The fact that their lineup included some of hip-hop's preeminent rappers and DJs didn't damage their standing.

Ice Cube left the fold in 1990 over a financial dispute, the first of many internal battles within N.W.A. The 1991 release *Efil4zaggin* (read it backward) outsold its predecessor and topped the charts. N.W.A. earned themselves a fresh spate of banning and condemnation of their efforts, all of which served to solidify their status as just the sort of bad boys the young record-buying public loves.

The delicate arrangement of personalities that was N.W.A. collapsed shortly thereafter, and Eazy-E became alienated from the group he had founded. Ice Cube established a thriving acting and rapping career. Dr. Dre went on to join the notorious Death Row Records camp, releasing the megahit *The Chronic* in 1992 and illustrating his condemnation of Eazy in a video that portrayed him as a greedy stooge in thrall to the group's manager. Eazy-E released the semi-self-explanatory *It's On (Dr. Dre) 187Um Killa* the next year.

N.W.A. dissolved in money-motivated rancor, and opportunities for the old friends to reconcile were dashed forever when Eazy-E was admitted to a Los Angeles hospital in 1995 for what he thought were asthma complications. A shocked Eric Wright was informed that he was suffering from late-stage AIDS and died a month later. N.W.A. would occasionally reunite by decade's end—older and considerably less angry at one another—but their roster would never again include their initial driving force.

Richey Edwards

1967–1995(?)

Manic Street Preachers' guitarist/vocalist Richey Edwards was a young artist who embraced the primacy of adolescent angst on an uncompromising scale. The Manics with Edwards were a band of lofty ambition and grand gestures, and his lyrics detailed his visions of greatness hand in hand with documentary accounts of his own slide into mental illness. On the eve of a 1995 promotional tour of the U.S., Edwards checked out of his London hotel and simply disappeared, never to be heard from again.

The Manics landed at the forefront of British rock with their 1992 release *Generation Terrorists*, which landed in the U.K. Top 20. Their music was incendiary and energetic, and they had a gift for controversy—bass player Nicky Wire told a concert audience that year he hoped Michael Stipe would go "the same way as Freddie Mercury pretty soon," and Edwards, during an interview, demonstrated his commitment to *something* by carving the phrase "4 real" into his arm. Subsequent releases would continue to land on the British charts, including 1994's *The Holy Bible*, in which Edwards detailed his flirtation with anorexia. He would enter a rehabilitation clinic that same year.

On February 1, 1995, Edwards checked out of London's Embassy Hotel. He left behind a packed suitcase, a bottle of Prozac, and a note reading "I Love You." Attempts to locate him produced nothing, and the police expressed the belief that he was probably dead. Two weeks later his Vauxhall Cavalier car was found abandoned. In his apartment were his passport, his Prozac prescription, his writings, and his credit cards. In a bizarre act of self-erasure, Manic Richey Edwards disappeared from the face of the earth. He has never been found.

ESSENTIAL LISTENING
Generation Terrorists

1934–1967

BRIAN
EPSTEIN

"Eight Days a Week"

Brian Epstein managed the Beatles through the first stage of their global domination, transforming a road-hardened four-piece into the world's most fabulous pop group. He controlled (or tried to) the Beatles's public image—how they dressed, what they said. A few years after their initial staggering success, the Beatles transformed from a simple pop group into a phenomenon that reflected and partially spurred the social tumult of the late sixties. Brian Epstein's strong paternal influence suddenly seemed very dated—a voice from another life, perhaps. Almost at the very moment the Beatles turned into a different beast, Brian Epstein died of a drug overdose. Suddenly the band was left to face reality without their erstwhile father figure, and their world would never be the same.

Epstein was a failed actor who was managing his father's NEMS record store in Liverpool when he got several requests for a German-import 7-inch called "My Bonnie," performed by Tony Sheridan with the Beat Brothers as backup. Epstein subsequently realized that the Beat Brothers were actually the Beatles and, as luck would have it, were performing at the local Cavern club just around the corner from NEMS.

Epstein checked out the Beatles at the Cavern Club and was impressed with their tight, dynamic sound (hardened by grueling gigging in Germany) and their ability to fire up a young lunchtime crowd. He soon became their manager, and compelled the boys to abandon their tough-guy leather jackets, jeans, and Brylcreem for suits and shampoo. Epstein had a vision of the Beatles as a mass success, and he was soon proved right when the group conquered the world.

Although the early Beatles seem sanitized and innocent in retrospect, the truth at the time was more complex. The designer suits and not-too-long, not-too-short haircuts the boys sported were calculated to put forth an image of safe-yet-sophisticated worldliness. They were clean-cut rebels, with an image that was acceptable to establishment society yet set them apart from bands that lacked their grooming and charm. It was a brilliant visual and marketing strategy. And it was Brian Epstein's doing.

Epstein was by most accounts a troubled man given to loneliness and depression. Much of his inner turmoil sprang from his closeted homosexuality, which was far from accepted in postwar Britain and carried with it the burden of possible legal consequences. Epstein had to hide the most pertinent fact of his personal life while the Beatles turned into a mass phenomenon and he became famous in his own right. Gradually, he had to deal with the fact that John, Paul, George, and Ringo were growing into men with their own viewpoints and opinions of how to be the Beatles.

Did the Beatles invent the sixties, or did the sixties invent the Beatles? It's a chicken-or-egg proposition. But by the 1966 the Beatles were no longer cuddly moptops enchanting the public with their whimsy and inventive love songs. They had endured John Lennon's "we're more popular than Jesus" controversy in America, and branched out with the groundbreaking explorations of *Rubber Soul* and *Revolver*. The release of *Sgt. Pepper's Lonely Hearts Club Band* in June 1967 permanently changed the musical landscape. Epstein was increasingly relegated to the sidelines by four young men who embodied a generation no longer seeking advice from their elders. The Beatles were in fact adrift themselves, but that wouldn't become clear until their fragmentation in the coming years.

On August 12 that year, the Beatles traveled to Wales to study Transcendental Meditation with the Maharishi Mahesh Yogi; by the end of the month Brian Epstein was dead of a drug overdose in his London bed. The Beatles reacted with shock and a dawning sense of having been abandoned in a crucial moment of their career. Brian Epstein had guided them through their early days, then succumbed when they became a different beast entirely. He's now remembered as a man who saw possibilities for pop music that no one had before.

Texan Roky Erickson's name is frequently evoked with Syd Barrett's and Peter Green's as sixties casualties whose drug experimentation led to fractured and fried minds and their disappearance from the music scene. Erickson surely did considerable damage to his own psyche through drug use, but his tale also involves tragic mishandling by the justice system and subsequent financial exploitation after his release from a mental hospital. While Barrett has permanently vanished from the public eye and Green has only recently resurfaced, Erickson has made several cult-level comebacks with varying degrees of success.

Erickson was a high school dropout who composed "You're Gonna Miss Me"—a garage prepunk classic that he recorded first with the Spades, then with the better-known 13th Floor Elevators. The latter version went to #56 in 1966, and the band signed with International Artists. The Elevators exemplified low-fi proto-grunge and whacked-out psychedelia, featuring Erickson's high-tenor vocals. They were also

ROKY ERICKSON

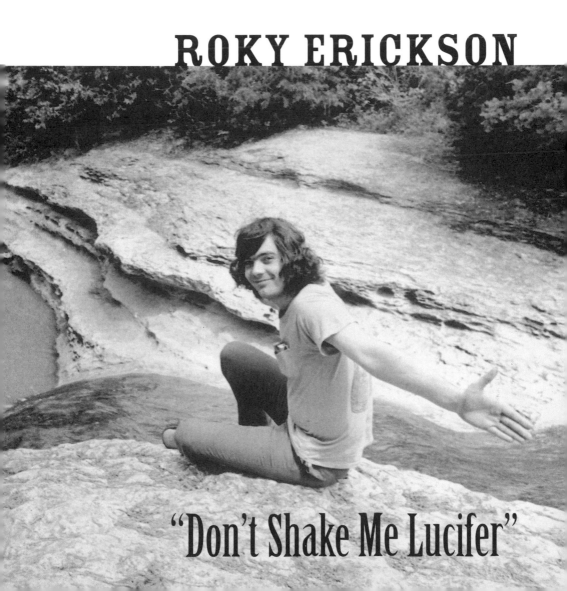

"Don't Shake Me Lucifer"

enthusiastic pot smokers and proponents of LSD use, which ensured negative attention from Texas authorities. In 1969 Erickson was arrested for possessing a joint; his lawyer suggested he plead insanity to escape jail time, but he was instead sentenced to three years at Rusk State Hospital for the criminally insane. There he was given electroshock therapy and powerful psychopharmaceuticals.

He was apparently never the same upon his release. He took up music again, but was soon exploited by deals in which he signed away royalties and publishing rights for little in return. Erickson earned a cult audience with titles such as "I Walk with a Zombie" and "Don't Shake Me Lucifer," and in 1982 signed an affidavit that he was "inhabited" by an alien. By the end of the eighties he had dropped out of music. In 1990 he was arrested for mail theft, but the charges were later dropped.

By the nineties Erickson was subsisting on a monthly Social Security check and suffering from continued mental instability that led to another stint in a mental institution. At the same time his profile as a cracked rock original continued to grow. 1990 saw the release of *Where the Pyramid Meets the Eye: A Tribute to Roky Erickson*, which saw acts such as R.E.M. and ZZ Top cover his material. Erickson released a new LP, *All That May Do My Rhyme*, in 1995 and a follow-up in 2000. Amid psychological turbulence, Erickson continued to occupy a small but distinctive niche in rock music.

While to some extent Erickson's fan base callously embraces him as a demented comedic figure, there is no denying the strange, enduring lunacy of his monster-movie-evoking paranoid garage music. Erickson's tale is lamentably serious, though, in view of the fact that he was essentially abused by the Texas legal and mental health establishments. For the crime of taking recreational drugs, Erickson had his mind wrecked. Cult-rocker status hardly seems a fitting recompense.

ESSENTIAL LISTENING
With 13th Floor Elevators:
Psychedelic Sounds of the 13th Floor Elevators
Solo: *All That May Do My Rhyme*

Bobby Fuller

"Never to Be Forgotten"

Bobby Fuller led the Bobby Fuller Four, a short-lived mid-sixties rock 'n' roll success formed in El Paso, Texas. After a regional hit, Fuller recorded a tune written by Sonny Curtis of Buddy Holly's Crickets called "I Fought the Law." The song was a compelling outlaw classic, and in 1966 it reached #9 on the charts. The Bobby Fuller Four followed up with a Buddy Holly cover for their next single, and while "Love's Made a Fool of You" didn't match the heights of its predecessor, it did make the Top 40.

There would not be another release from Bobby Fuller; on July 18, 1965, Fuller died in Los Angeles, his body found in his car in front of his home. He had been severely beaten, and had apparently ingested gasoline. The police nonetheless ruled Fuller's death a suicide. Fuller's friends insisted that he had been menaced recently by local mobsters, possibly in connection with a woman. Fuller's death has never been adequately explained, and probably never will be.

After Fuller's death the band transformed into the Randy Fuller Four, with brother Randy at the helm. Chart success eluded them. "I Fought the Law" would eventually be covered by the Clash—it was, in fact, their first record officially released in America, in 1979.

marvin GAYE JR.

1939–1984

"Trouble Man"

I f sweet soul music and sultry hymns to sexuality were your poison, you weren't going to do any better than Marvin Gaye. A pity, then, that Gaye's own poisons were considerably stronger; he supplemented his musical genius with a lifestyle that comprised hearty doses of hard drugs and a downward spiral of craziness that ultimately led to one of the most sorrowful deaths in rock history. A man beset by demons, Gaye's bizarre drug-induced behavior finally compelled a member of his closest family to kill Marvin in self-defense.

when she collapsed onstage in 1967 and was diagnosed with a brain tumor. The pair continued to record successfully, but Terrell's eventual death in 1970 after a string of unsuccessful surgeries left Gaye severely despondent and led to his temporary retreat from the public eye.

Gaye opened up R&B to political themes of peace, poverty, and environmental degradation on 1971's *What's Going On* LP, and enjoyed a string of further critical and commercial success into the seventies, but as the decade wore on his personal problems began to overwhelm him. In 1976 he faced a short jail sentence for

...an argument between Gaye and his father... turned deadly when father shot son.

Marvin Gaye was shot dead by his father on April 1, 1984, following a violent argument in the Crenshaw, Los Angeles, house that Gaye had bought for his parents after his chart-topping success in the sixties. Saddled with a debilitating drug addiction, Gaye had become delusional and erratic in the years before his death, and his killing by Marvin Sr. culminated a startling personal decline.

Gaye was one of Motown's greatest artists, lending a dynamic presence and crystalline voice to hits such as "Stubborn Kind of Fellow," "How Sweet It Is (To Be Loved by You)," "What's Going On," and "Let's Get It On." In the mid-sixties he enjoyed a string of hit duets with Tammi Terrell, although tragedy struck

contempt of court after failing to pay alimony and child support to wife Anna Gordy, sister of Motown founder Berry Gordy. Gaye and Anna divorced, and Gaye found himself beset by the IRS for a tax bill that reached seven figures. His personal behavior became more unpredictable, and his drug intake increased—particularly of freebase cocaine, which would eventually develop into an all-consuming habit. Gaye collapsed onstage in November 1978, and by February of the next year he retreated to Maui, where he reportedly lived in a trailer and attempted suicide by drug overdose.

By the early eighties, Gaye's performances became more infrequent and erratic, and he began to suffer from paranoia and delusions as

Why Bother Playing the Game After *That*?

In 1983, a year before his death, Gaye sang the national anthem at the NBA All-Star game in Los Angeles. Eschewing the usual stodgy renditions of the song favored by middle school choirs and middling country singers, Gaye turned *"The Star Spangled Banner"* into a slow soul jam complete with vocal histrionics and baroque twists and turns that rendered the song's actual melody a distant memory. Depending on the listener's perspective, it was an act of either sheer genius or addled eccentricity. Cameras in the arena captured the All-Stars themselves looking on with wide eyes, a few straining not to laugh. In retrospect, many consider it a classic moment in R&B history.

Hey, That Football Player Looks Like . . .

Following Tammi Terrell's 1970 death, Gaye went into a period of personal turmoil that included a sudden determination that he would become a pro football player for the Detroit Lions. Gaye was out of shape, but he went on a rigorous exercise program and bulked up with more than twenty-five pounds of muscle. The Lions apparently talked Gaye out of a tryout on grounds of liability and insurance. If nothing else, though, Gaye was in great shape and entered into a prolific period of his career.

a result of years of hard drug abuse. He made a comeback in 1982 with the hit single "Sexual Healing" and LP *Midnight Love*, although that same year he had to sell his one-million-dollar home in order to continue paying off his tax bill. In 1983 Gaye went on a final tour that featured a string of sellout shows, although by this time his drug consumption had taken over and death threats during the course of the tour eroded his already tenuous hold on sanity.

In November 1983, Gaye moved into his parents' house—not a great idea for any adult, much less one whose personality was slipping off the rails. He would find himself quickly ensnared in old conflicts with his Apostolic preacher father, whose effeminacy and propensity for physical and verbal abuse had caused young Marvin consternation and confusion during his youth. In fact, his adding of an "e" to the family name "Gay" was an early attempt at allaying any questions about his masculinity. Gaye's conflicted consciousness was thrown into turmoil by his return home, where his childhood confusion between the "virtue" of religion and the "vice" of sensuality plunged him deeper into guilt, anxiety, and paranoia.

By this point Gaye's hold on reality and his muse had disintegrated under the weight of freebase addiction, and in March of the next year he began to announce to relatives that he planned to take his own life. At one point a gun was forcibly removed from his hand during a spell of disoriented raving. On April 1, an argument between Gaye and his father on a Sunday morning turned deadly when father shot son. Marvin Gaye, Sr., was sentenced to five years in prison for voluntary manslaughter, and Marvin Gaye's ashes were lowered into the sea by Anna and Marvin's three children.

Gaye's musical legacy has lived on, and his music has maintained a steady popularity as trends have come and gone. His demise seems to have been kept at arm's length from his recorded work, which still articulates themes of love, sensuality, and social awareness. He is best remembered more as the impossibly smooth singer that he once was, rather than the sad figure that he eventually became.

ROCK AND ROLL HALL OF FAME
Inducted 1987

A PARTING GIFT, PERHAPS

In 1979 Marvin Gaye released the double LP *Here, My Dear*. It was a concept piece about the breakup of Gaye's marriage to Anna Gordy, with an added twist: The judge in their divorce ordered profits from the record to be passed directly to Anna. Gaye was by then hardly a model of fiduciary responsibility, and this was the court's way of ensuring that Anna received a financial settlement. Strangely, given the circumstances, *Here, My Dear* was an excellent record with moments of true brilliance.

1945–1979

Lowell George
"It's So Easy to Slip"

Of all the nearly forgotten gems of the seventies, Little Feat's output ranks among the most accomplished and overlooked. With a deceptively easygoing sound, Little Feat impeccably fused blues, snaky funk, country, and R&B into songs that rarely failed to feature an unexpected twist or surreal turn. Behind many of these hijinks was Lowell George, whose shambling career was spiked with moments of brilliance. After years of breakups and re-formations with Little Feat, George struck out on his own but was felled by a heart attack while touring to support his first solo album.

George was a natural musician who played flute at Hollywood High School and soon after played saxophone on recordings by Frank Sinatra. In the mid-seventies he joined Frank Zappa's Mothers of Invention as guitarist and vocalist on such twisted classics as *Hot Rats* and *Weasels Ripped My Flesh*. Zappa was impressed with George's songwriting talents and suggested he start his own band. George commented that this was "a nice way of firing me, I think."

Little Feat was formed and, over the course of the next few years, George's versatile roots vocals and slide guitar moved to the fore of the group's sound. A run of albums—*Sailin' Shoes*,

Dixie Chicken, and *Feats Don't Fail Me Now*—became cult classics. The band released the classic "Willin'," a tongue-in-cheek truck driver's blues, and "Easy to Slip." Still, Little Feat met with limited success, and as the decade wore on drew much of its revenue from touring and various members' session work.

By the late seventies, George was drifting away from the group. Personnel instability and disorganization resulted in Little Feat's continued inability to capitalize on what opportunities they were afforded. George himself was a notoriously inept businessman—one report has him playing a session for free because he was in a hurry to use the studio. He gradually became more involved with drugs, and developed a reputation as a near recluse and gifted underdog whose greatest talent was inadvertently evading fame and fortune.

By decade's end George dissolved Little Feat altogether (they would re-form in a new incarnation in 1988) and released a solo LP, *Thanks, I'll Eat It Here*. He formed a band and went on tour, but died of a heart attack on June 29, 1979. The early days of Little Feat have failed to become a classic-rock radio staple, but the lasting quality of their records is capable of surprising listeners even today.

"I Can't Help It"

It would scarcely be unfair to say that Andy Gibb had the world handed to him on a platter—he was lucky enough to come of age at the precise moment when megastardom was the Gibb family business. Rock 'n' roll fame and success came quickly and easily to him, but slipped away just as rapidly amid a quagmire of cocaine and alcohol. An alarming decline and early death followed. Friends and family recall Gibb as affable and kind, memories that amplify the tragic aspects of his fleeting moment of glory. In fact, Andy Gibb was that particular brand of rock 'n' roll casualty whose appetites got the better of him; simply put, he ran himself into the grave with his addictions.

Andy Gibb grew up in Australia under the shadow of his older brothers Barry, Maurice, and Robin, who plied their musical trade as the Bee Gees (as in Brothers Gibb). The elder Gibb brothers enjoyed a string of international hits in the sixties, and Andy grew up witnessing rock stardom from a front-row perspective. He must have liked what he saw, because by the mid-seventies he was recording and performing in Australia—one tour had him supporting the tartan-fetishizing Bay City Rollers.

ANDY GIBB

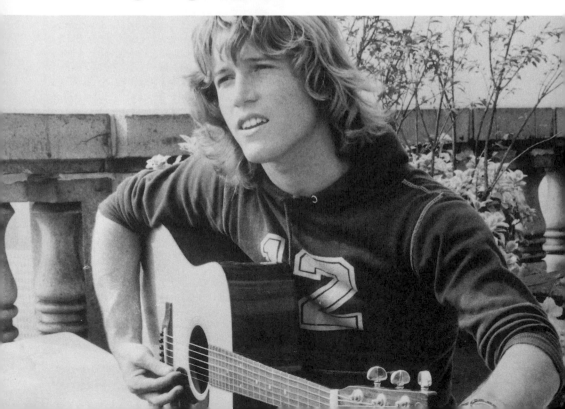

The early seventies were a dire and fallow period for the Bee Gees, but their fortunes improved considerably as the decade progressed. In 1977 Andy, at big brother Barry's urging, signed on with the Bee Gees's record label, RSO. Recorded in a two-day session, the Barry-penned "I Just Want to Be Your Everything" became a #1 hit in America. Andy Gibb became a teen pinup star around the world, with his good looks, million-dollar smile, and easygoing charisma.

The next year, 1978, was one that the Gibb family must look back upon with fondness. The *Saturday Night Fever* soundtrack, which featured seven songs by the Bee Gees, would eventually sell thirty million copies. A rising tide tends to lift all boats, and Andy Gibb's was raised very high indeed; he enjoyed two more #1s with "(Love Is) Thicker than Water" and "Shadow Dancing." Andy sang much like his brothers, and his music was predominantly written and produced by them as well. As a result, a ubiquitous Gibb sound permeated the airwaves in 1978. Andy possessed genuine star quality, but it didn't hurt that his elder brothers had a stranglehold on the late-seventies zeitgeist, and were prolific enough to pass along perfectly crafted gems to their teen-idol younger brother.

The fall of the Bee Gees set in almost immediately thereafter. Although they still enjoyed chart hits for a time, their appearance in the universally scorned film *Sgt. Pepper's Lonely Hearts Club Band* initiated the derailment of their career (and managed to drag down Peter Frampton as well). Andy enjoyed a few hits over the next couple of years—including duets with fellow late-seventies icon Olivia Newton-John—but by 1982 Gibb's viability as a recording artist had pretty much become a thing of the past. He then began a second career as a professional celebrity.

Gibb was a staple on television talk shows, his relaxed likeability masking a cocaine addiction that worsened in the coming years. While he remained the same charming Andy during shifts of sobriety, when he drank and abused drugs he was increasingly troubled and erratic. In 1982 he scuttled a gig hosting the popular music-TV show *Solid Gold,* getting himself fired after missing several tapings. He then landed a starring role in a production of *Joseph and the Amazing Technicolor Dreamcoat;* later he was sacked after missing a dozen performances in a single

month. Then Andy went on *Good Morning America* and publicly admitted he was a drug addict.

Gibb tried a couple of stints in rehab, including a stay at the Betty Ford Clinic in 1985. But his conditioned worsened, much to the consternation and despair of his friends and family. He endured the addict's painful cycles of sobriety and bingeing, and his brothers in particular looked on in dismay. The Bee Gees had set up a new home base in Miami, and from there they hoped to spark a renaissance for the entire clan; Andy himself received a ray of hope in early 1988 in the form of a deal with Island Records. At the time the contract seemed like a godsend, for Andy had seen his personal fortune whittled down to nothing, having filed for bankruptcy.

A projected return to pop stardom turned out to be a painful trial for Andy. He recorded tracks under the ever-steadfast tutelage of Barry, but ran aground when compelled to compose songs to flesh out his projected album. Andy retreated to brother Robin's country estate in England and collided with a massive writer's block. The truth was that Andy had never been much of a songwriter on his own, and the pressure of coming up with new material plunged him into a depressive tailspin. Amid this anxiety and fear of failure, Andy was admitted to a hospital on March 7 with severe stomach pains; he died three days later, suddenly, of heart failure. Some erroneous reports would claim that Gibb died of an overdose, but the reality seemed to be that he had succumbed to damage self-inflicted by years of cocaine and alcohol abuse. He died five days after his thirtieth birthday, leaving painful memories of a young man who was unable to control his addictions and who paid the highest price as a result.

ESSENTIAL LISTENING
Solo: A Collection of His Greatest Hits

The Grateful DEAD

Jerry Garcia
1942–1995

ROCK AND ROLL HALL OF FAME
Inducted 1994

Theirs was a world of free-form musical trip-outs, hard-core hippies, and whirling dervishes enjoying a moment of bliss while on leave from their day jobs. The Grateful Dead's trip was indeed long and strange: musically, the Dead forged a sound both roots-based and experimental, traditional one moment and avant-garde the next. They also consumed a mountain of drugs and a river of alcohol, which played no small part in the losses that befell the band throughout its tenure. The permanent end came when Jerry Garcia, the Dead's heart and soul, finally succumbed to the ravages of drug addiction. Fans would also endlessly speculate whether the group's keyboard seat was cursed, after three deaths spanning almost twenty years. Like them or not—and they always had a knack for eliciting strong reactions—the Dead were an American cultural phenomenon to be reckoned with, and their story was as many-colored as the tie-dyed T-shirts their adherents sported.

The Dead were formed by San Francisco Bay Area natives; they were initially a jug band, but took on a rock flavor in the mid-sixties. Settling on their name after a stint as the Warlocks, the Grateful Dead found themselves

"Such a Long Long Time to Be Gone"

located at the epicenter of the psychedelic hippie moment. They became an integral part of the scene, playing at author Ken Kesey's Acid Tests—surrealist semipublic events revolving around the participants' ingestion of LSD. Acid, for the moment, was still legal, and it heavily influenced the nascent Dead's music and worldview. A move to the Haight-Ashbury district of San Francisco cemented their place at the center of sixties youth culture.

Jerome John Garcia—Jerry to his friends—was the son of a 1930s big-band leader. Jerry possessed a vast familiarity with the American music vernacular, and was a gifted guitarist with a distinctive style that in time developed into one of rock's great signature sounds. He formed the original nucleus of the Dead with guitarist Bob Weir, bass player Phil Lesh, drummer Bill Kreutzmann, and organist and harmonica player Ron "Pigpen" McKernan (anyone nicknamed "Pigpen" probably should give up on ever being called "Ron" again, as McKernan learned). A second drummer, Mickey Hart, was added in 1967. The band soon developed a reputation as one that had to be seen live to be understood—their shows included original material, covers, and improvised instrumental freak-outs that were most appreciated by audiences under the influence of drugs.

Along the way, the Dead developed into a tight unit, with its central band members becoming almost telepathic in their musical rapport. They were crucial to the Bay Area sixties scene, playing benefits and free concerts, and maintaining a visible presence at their 710 Ashbury Street headquarters. They also for a time managed to avoid getting rich from their cult success and heavy touring—upon the release of their third LP, *Aoxomoxoa*, they owed Warner Brothers one hundred thousand dollars and another album. Wisely deciding that it was time to bring in a professional, in 1969 the Dead retained famed promoter Bill Graham to handle their concert bookings. It was the beginning of the Dead's mining the road for cash, which would in time make them all very wealthy men.

But no one should infer that the Grateful Dead, by the end of the sixties, were meta-morphosing into straitlaced businessmen. The band was busted for pot in New Orleans—eventually turning the experience into the classic tune "Truckin'." The same year the group discovered that their business manager had been embezzling money. Drug consumption for the Dead continued with the hearty regularity with which mere mortals interface with air and food. Their audiences also indulged, sometimes unintentionally: In 1971 fans needed medical treatment after unknowingly consuming acid-laced cider at a San Francisco show. The group recorded and toured extensively throughout the seventies, produced a dizzying parade of side projects and offshoots, and generally carried the torch they had lit more than a decade previously.

The Grateful Dead were always more than just a band, no matter the decade; they were also an ongoing philosophical experiment. They constantly encroached upon the fuzzy border between tradition and experimentation in their music, they exemplified personal exploration and alternative lifestyles for their legion of fans, and they walked a line between hippie idealism and the American profit margin. This was a potent mix of ambitions and ideologies, and along the way, the Grateful Dead suffered the inevitable casualties. The first was the man with the barnyard nickname.

Pigpen had grown up enamored with the blues and R&B; by high school he was learning guitar, piano, and harmonica. He was an integral part of the Dead's basis in American roots music—country, blues, and folk—and contributed piano and harmonica to the fecund cosmic stew of the band's early years. But whereas the Dead and their San Francisco contemporaries heartily embraced psychedelics, Pigpen McKernan preferred the oblivion granted by the bottle. By 1970, at the age of twenty-five, Pigpen's health had started to deteriorate. He was diagnosed with advanced liver disease and ordered to stop drinking. The Dead were forced to hire an additional keyboard player, Keith Godchaux. Although Pigpen tried to resume his duties with the band, his liver was beyond repair. He died on March 8, 1973, of a stomach hemorrhage and liver failure. Godchaux's wife, Donna, also joined the permanent lineup as a backup vocalist.

ESSENTIAL LISTENING
A tricky prospect, since the Dead were always more effective onstage than on recordings. Their best studio work can be found on *American Beauty* and *Workingman's Dead*. Live recordings under the *Dick's Picks* series have been aficionado-approved and represent all eras of the Dead's journey.

An All-Around Friend
In the mid-sixties the Dead had a famous (or notorious, depending on your point of view) benefactor in Owsley Stanley, better known for being one of the largest manufacturers and distributors of the still-legal hallucinogen LSD. Stanley also designed a high-tech sound system for the boys.

Ron "Pigpen" McKernan
1945–1973

By the late seventies the Dead largely abandoned attempts at locating bliss in the recording studio. Although they had enjoyed some semihits such as "Uncle John's Band," "Casey Jones," "Box of Rain," and "Alabama Getaway," their bread-and-butter means of sustenance was spending half their time on the road. Keith and Donna Godchaux left the fold in 1979, with the keyboard seat taken by Brent Mydland. The next year, Keith was hurt badly when his car collided with a flatbed truck in the Bay Area; he died two days later.

The eighties were a seriously mixed affair for the Grateful Dead. Improbably, their tours became major events. They drew larger and larger crowds everywhere they went. They put out no new recordings, yet became more popular than ever before. Their hard-core fan base of Deadheads was augmented by hordes of newcomers: college kids, white-collar types looking for an antidote to the forty-hour work grind, and curious first-timers. Purists shuddered at the sight of frat boys tripping out to "Dark Star," but the Dead themselves enjoyed success on a scale previously unimagined. And they seemed to retain their integrity in the process: They employed a large staff like a family business, and embraced their fans by encouraging the practice of plugging into mixing desks to make free concert bootlegs.

But the dark side was never far away. With larger audiences came trouble never seen before in mellow Dead crowds. In 1989, fifty-five people were arrested at two Pittsburgh shows, then seventy more at concerts in Irvine. In October of the same year, a college student died of a broken neck outside a Dead show in New Jersey. Two months later, another fan, high on LSD, died in police custody in Los Angeles.

Worse, there was deep trouble at the very core of the band. During this period of commercial resurgence Jerry Garcia was slipping deeper and deeper into heroin addiction. In 1985 Jerry was busted in San Francisco's Golden Gate Park; at the band's urging Jerry sought rehab treatment. The next year Jerry fell into a frightening diabetic coma that lasted five days. Always a big man, he was putting on more and more weight, chain-smoking, and relapsing into addiction. Friends began to openly worry about his condition.

Keith Godchaux 1948–1980

Brent Mydland 1953–1990

In 1987 the Dead pulled off a coup that few thought them capable of—they made a hit record. *In the Dark* went Top 10, as did its single "Touch of Grey." It was a high-water mark for the Dead—their concerts were still selling out and, for once, they were touring on the back of a successful album. The Dead's performances became more erratic during this mainstream popularity, however, depending on the daily status of Jerry's health. The undertow of drug use shook the band hard in 1990, when Brent Mydland died of an injection of morphine and cocaine. He was the third Grateful Dead keyboardist to die.

In the early nineties years of drug abuse and hard living were taking their toll on Jerry Garcia. Fans watched his progress with anxiety, monitoring his weight and gauging his well-being by the quality of his guitar playing. In 1995, the invisible threads that held together the Grateful Dead finally gave way. Ominous portents came on a final tour, when three concertgoers were struck by lightning at JFK Stadium and more than a hundred fans were injured when a deck collapsed at a show in Missouri. On August 9 the world received stunning news: Jerry Garcia had died.

A month after playing a final concert in Chicago, Jerry had quietly checked himself into a drug rehab center in northern California. At Serenity Knolls, trying one more time to kick the addictions that had dogged him for more than a decade, Jerry was found dead in his sleep. Attempts by a nurse and a paramedic to revive Jerry failed. The coroner indicated that Jerry had died of a heart attack caused by hardening of the arteries, although the same report also suggested that Jerry had used heroin the day before he died.

By year's end the Grateful Dead issued a statement indicating they were officially finished. The remaining band members reconfigured in various new guises, touring and recording with a much lower profile than they had previously enjoyed. Improbably enough, the Dead had endured for three decades; now it was time to pack it in. They could survive the loss of three keyboard players, but without Jerry they were no longer the Dead.

🏆 **ROCK AND ROLL HALL OF FAME**
Fleetwood Mac inducted 1998

PETER GREEN

"The Green Manalishi (With the Two-Prong Crown)"

Although most music fans know well the Fleetwood Mac of *Rumours* and *The Dance*, fewer outside Britain recall the band's first life as a leading force in late-sixties blues-rock. Leading the way in Fleetwood Mac's early days was guitarist Peter Green, an inventive and soulful blues player who was considered on a par with the greatest of his time. Drugs and mental instability dogged his career, however, and after leaving the band he would endure a stay in a mental hospital and years of seclusion. In an unlikely and encouraging turn, though, by the end of the nineties Green had returned to the stage and was managing an attempt at reviving his career.

Green got his start in John Mayall's Bluesbreakers, along with bandmates Mick Fleetwood and John McVie. Along with guitarist Jeremy Spencer the four formed Fleetwood Mac in 1967. Green both sang and played guitar, and the band quickly generated a repertoire of blues material that led to a series of U.K. hits including "Black Magic Woman" and "Albatross." The band failed to rise to the top

of their field in America despite a few tours here, but they enjoyed considerable stardom in their native Britain.

A couple of years later things started to turn weird for Green. He lapsed into deep depressions, and bemoaned the spiritual emptiness of rock 'n' roll. The song "Oh Well" was released at the end of 1969, and it reflected Green's inner turmoil as he moved away from his Jewish heritage towards Christianity. Simultaneously, he began wearing long white robes onstage, writing very large checks to charities, and suggesting to Fleetwood Mac that they henceforth must donate their proceeds to good works—an idea the band rejected.

Green had dabbled with LSD, and it had strongly affected his view of the world. In Munich in 1969, Fleetwood Mac went to an after-gig party at a house owned by some wealthy fans. After a short time there, the band realized that they had been dosed with acid. Green stayed at the commune for several days, even declaring to his bandmates his wish to relocate there permanently. He was pried away, but his introspection and self-absorption deepened after several days of tripping on LSD. Soon his playing began to reflect the consciousness of a man losing touch with reality. "Peter Green was never the same after that," Mick Fleetwood said.

Early the next year the band recorded a Green composition called "The Green Manalishi (With the Two-Prong Crown)" that, while eventually a Top 10 hit in the U.K., reflected Green's inner struggles with harrowing intensity. A song of hallucinatory anxiety and the despair of madness, it was the sound of a man losing his mind. By April 1970, Green had quit Fleetwood Mac. A month later "Green Manalishi" climbed the charts.

At the end of the year Green released a solo LP, *In the End of the Game* (a Top 40 British hit), that was essentially his attempt at capturing the psychedelic-influenced labyrinth of his thoughts. Meanwhile Fleetwood Mac carried on without Green—though they suffered another strange defection in 1971, when Jeremy Spencer abruptly quit to join the religious cult the Children of God. These were strange days of psychedelic fallout, and Peter Green spent some time on an Israeli kibbutz before returning to England for menial jobs that included digging graves and working as a hospital orderly. He'd given away nearly all his possessions by this point, and bounced around on friends' sofas. He was suffering from hallucinations and delusions, and was given pharmaceutical treatment and electroshock therapy. Those who knew him say that Green seemed frightened and lost.

In 1977, Green made an apparently facetious threat to former manager Clifford Davis over some old royalties—by now, Green was living an essentially hand-to-mouth existence. Davis decided not to take lightly a threat from the unstable Green, and after he phoned the police, Green was sent to Brixton Prison and subsequently to a psychiatric hospital. He was officially diagnosed a schizophrenic at the same moment

his old band, reconstituted with Stevie Nicks and Lindsey Buckingham, was beginning to enjoy phenomenal success with its *Rumours* LP.

In 1980 Green released a new solo LP, which again hit the Top 40 in the U.K., but soon he disappeared once more from the public eye. He spent the eighties in obscurity, and rumors and tales of his disorganized lifestyle filtered into the music press. He had apparently lost his faculty on the guitar, and was reduced to a semihomeless lifestyle of near poverty. It was a sad story of a considerable talent brought low by mental illness, and Peter Green began to take on the legend of a rock 'n' roll casualty.

But in the nineties Green's fortunes improved somewhat. He reemerged from the fog of the previous decade and was housed and cared for by friends. With their encouragement, he began to play the guitar again and reacquaint himself with the instrument. By the mid-nineties he had returned to the stage and recording studio with a new band, the Splinter Group. Although in interviews it was clear that Green was a man with a delicate hold on his psyche, he seemed to have stabilized and attained some degree of equanimity, if not contentment. So, for now, Peter Green's story finds the reclusive legend again delicately testing the waters of musical notoriety. From public statements he seems well aware that he simply cannot handle the pressures of fame on any large scale, and is determined to ply his craft on a level he can manage. Hopefully, he will be able to do just that; one senses that now, for Peter Green, playing rock 'n' roll is not a game of topping the charts and conquering the world. It has become a matter of expressing himself and surviving.

ESSENTIAL LISTENING
Fleetwood Mac: *The Original Fleetwood Mac (Original Recording Remastered)*
Solo: *Green and Guitar: The Best of Peter Green*
In the End of the Game

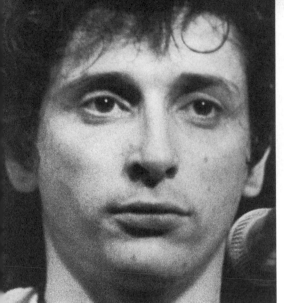

Johnny Thunders
1952–1991

"You Can't Put Your Arms Around a Memory"

Jerry Nolan
1946–1992

 ESSENTIAL LISTENING
Johnny Thunders and the Heartbreakers:
Live at Max's Kansas City '79

The Heartbreakers

The Heartbreakers (no, *not* Tom Petty's backing band, and they must have gotten very tired of explaining that fact) formed in New York in the mid-seventies. Johnny Thunders had played in cult favorites the New York Dolls, and he was joined by Richard Hell, formerly of CBGB's-haunting Television. Guitarist Walter Lure and drummer Jerry Nolan filled out a lineup that quickly became known in New York as one of the great punk-rock bands. The Heartbreakers played loud and fast, with the sneering Thunders exemplifying the rocker-junkie onstage and off, and drew comparisons with the decadence and aggression of the Rolling Stones in their prime.

If the Heartbreakers had formed and gigged in, say, Oklahoma City, they would probably have broken up and been forgotten. But they had the good fortune to play in New York, where their audiences included many critics hungry for an antidote to seventies progressive/corporate rock. The Heartbreakers eventually toured Britain, where they encountered the Clash, the Sex Pistols, and the Damned. Thunders and company blazed a decadent trail wherever they went, with Thunders in full embrace of heroin. While in England the Heartbreakers recorded 1977's *L.A.M.F.*; the record sounded so terrible to his ears that drummer Nolan quit the group. Thunders went on to record the solo *So Alone* the next year. The release sold very little but was duly placed on music critics' record shelves everywhere.

It wasn't the Heartbreakers's fault they were critical darlings, though, and their uncompromising path certainly ensured them the hardships that come to those who spurn convention and conformity. Thunders, the stalwart Heartbreaker, in particular embodied a balls-out rock ideal that he took to his grave. The Heartbreakers would go on to reconvene sporadically, playing a final show together in 1990. The next year Thunders toured Japan and, upon his return, died in a New Orleans hotel from an overdose of methadone and alcohol. Nolan had suffered for some time from ailments springing from drug use, and he died in 1992. Johnny Thunders and the Heartbreakers definitely made some rude, brash noise, the sort that drove a few dinosaurs out to pasture. For that we thank them.

1942–1970

Jimi Hendrix

"Voodoo Chile"

He had the distinction of being the best electric guitar player in rock 'n' roll history—a vocation and craft that millions have taken up since Les Paul invented the solid-body guitar in 1941. No matter who they are, how well they have played, and however many discs they have recorded, guitar players all know that—at best—they will take second place in history to James Marshall Hendrix. Hendrix's death from drugs was a senseless loss that, ironically, permanently fixed his position as the unassailable master of rock guitar. No twelve-bar, half hearted phone-in efforts were to come from a middle-aged Hendrix, and no flogging the small-theater circuit before audiences rapt with hope for a glimpse of his former genius. While we feel the loss of the possible heights he might have scaled, the new frontiers he might have mapped like a musical Magellan, he also left a legacy of unimpeachable greatness and innovation that decades of posthumous releases have failed to tarnish.

Jimi Hendrix was from Seattle, and started playing guitar when he was a boy. After he turned eighteen he joined the army, spending three years as a member of the Screaming Eagles paratrooper squad before breaking his ankle on his twenty-sixth and final parachute jump. One might wonder what Hendrix absorbed from all those free-fall plunges to earth, and how the experience might have influenced his dive-bomb runs on the guitar by the end of the sixties. For the time being, though, the young Hendrix played the American R&B club circuit. Though only in his early twenties, he was already sharp and professional enough to meet the stringent demands of backing Curtis Mayfield and the Impressions, Sam Cooke, Curtis Knight, Jackie Wilson, Little Richard, Hank Ballard, the Supremes, and the Isley Brothers.

By 1966 Hendrix had formed his own group; that summer the Animals's Chas Chandler saw Jimi play at Cafe Wha? in Greenwich Village, and suggested that swinging London would be an appropriate venue for Jimi's blossoming talent. In England Jimi hooked up with drummer Mitch Mitchell and bass player Noel Redding to form Hendrix's classic trio, the Jimi Hendrix Experience. In October they hit the studio and recorded the psychedelic blues "Hey Joe."

Suddenly the right mix was found. Hendrix's apprenticeship in American blues and R&B collided with the sonic experimentalism ushered in by the Beatles's *Revolver* and the mind-warping effects of LSD (still legal at the time). But speaking of Jimi's music as the sum of its parts misses the point by a mile—it's tantamount to describing the taste of a hallucinogenic mushroom before the effects begin to kick in. The guitar, in Jimi's hands, began to express things no one had ever imagined before. It seemed to cry for reasons too complex to understand, to lust for the sensuality coursing through myth and poetry, and to exult in violence and peace within the same run of notes. In short, Jimi Hendrix started to blow people's minds.

In 1967 "Hey Joe" charted #7 in the U.K. Hendrix, aflame with energy and invention onstage, began to play the guitar with his teeth and set it on fire—all the while creating sonic mind bombs with the use of distortion and feedback. In May "Purple Haze" was released, then the album *Are You Experienced?* Both upped the ante considerably. The next month the Experience made its U.S. debut at the Monterey Pop Festival, where performances of "Wild Thing" and "Like a Rolling Stone" stunned the audience. Hendrix's next album, *Axis: Bold as Love,* would eventually reach #3 in the U.S.

Hendrix was firmly gripping a cosmic live wire with both hands; he ingested all the musical experimentation around him and disgorged it in new, unforeseen ways. The next album, *Electric Ladyland*, mapped new terrain by resurrecting Dylan's folky "All Along the Watchtower" as a Frankenstein's monster of soaring ups and downs and apocalyptic storms. "Voodoo Chile" reeked of a similar menace, as Hendrix expressed the psychic turbulence ripening beneath the flower-power bliss of the sixties. As always, it was his guitar that led the way—although he was also developing into a surprisingly emotive and textured singer.

But Jimi Hendrix's expression of the darkness, a deep-rooted psychedelic blues that he alone was capable of creating, may well have also been a manifestation of an inner bleakness intensified by his drug use. It was a tricky business, drugs, in the sixties—experimentation was de rigueur, and the possibility that usage might lead to mental imbalance or foster problems of the same grand scope as the insights they brought forth from the unconscious was barely acknowledged, or was pushed under the carpet. In May 1969, Hendrix was arrested for heroin possession in Toronto; he was subsequently found not guilty. There's no doubt, though, that at the end of the decade Hendrix was descending the slippery slide from dabbling to full-fledged abuse. He wasn't alone. Like so many other rock stars, Hendrix attained fame quickly, and he felt the demands of his muse were all-consuming. The wide-open vistas of his creativity started to narrow with disillusionment and spiritual fatigue.

In 1969 Hendrix disbanded the Experience; at the end of the year he debuted his new group, Band of Gypsys. A New Year's Eve 1970 show was released as a double LP, but by the end of January Hendrix walked offstage at Madison Square Garden in the middle of their second song of the night. Band of Gypsys was no more. Hendrix embarked on a tour, but reports of his shows that spring and summer were mixed. In July he played a homecoming gig in Seattle where he reportedly insulted the audience. Two months later, he left a Denmark stage with the words "I've been dead for a long time" in response to a disappointed heckler.

On September 18, Hendrix was in a death spiral. He left a message on Chas Chandler's answering machine: "I need help bad, man." When the clock was about to strike midnight, Hendrix was pronounced dead on arrival at St. Mary Abbot's Hospital in London. The cause of his demise was inhalation of his own vomit due to intense barbiturate intoxication. His body was returned to Washington for burial. The coroner did not rule out suicide in Hendrix's case, but no firm conclusion was ever reached. What we know with certainty is that Jimi Hendrix went supernova in a solo recording career that lasted less than four years. Since his death more than one hundred albums have been released under Hendrix's name—some good, some rehashing previously released material, others representing a dredge through every studio outtake and misfire Hendrix ever committed to tape. In truth, there were no lost masterpieces to rival the output of Hendrix's lifetime. But there will always be a hunger for more of his transcendent genius, for the sound of a man going so far *out there* that no one could bring him back.

ESSENTIAL LISTENING
Are You Experienced?
Electric Ladyland

ROCK AND ROLL HALL OF FAME
Inducted 1992

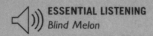
Shannon Hoon

"Deserted"

O ne-hit wonder Blind Melon fused acoustic rock, seventies guitar play, and Grateful Dead–styled airiness into an unabashedly retro sound in the early nineties. They were formed in Los Angeles, where after only a week of playing together they received major-label interest and soon secured a deal. Before Blind Melon's first release, vocalist Shannon Hoon sang backup for fellow Indiana native Axl Rose on Guns N' Roses' *Use Your Illusion* double set. Upon the release of *Blind Melon* the group became a platinum success on the strength of the #1 "No Rain," a fairly innocuous tune that became well known partly on the strength of the "bee girl" featured in its video. Lasting pursuit of rock bliss would not follow, however, for on October 21, 1995, Hoon succumbed to a drug overdose while the band was touring to support sophomore LP *Soup*. Blind Melon were derided in their day as derivative and lightweight, but in contrast to the boy bands that followed a few years later they seem positively steeped in authenticity. Surviving band members pledged to continue without Hoon, but by 1999 they admitted defeat and broke up permanently.

MICHAEL HUTCHENCE

He apparently had it all: glamour, fame, money, and a tight-knit band. So what happened? Michael Hutchence was one of the biggest rock stars of the eighties, fronting INXS to a series of huge pop hits and in the process becoming an international jet-setter. Although the nineties saw INXS explore the gradual downhill career trajectory of a band going out of fashion but still capable at its craft, Hutchence remained on the surface every bit the living-large rock icon, romancing British celebrity Paula Yates and fathering a daughter. So it was a deep shock to the world when, in 1997, Hutchence's body was found hanging from a door hinge in an Australian hotel room. (More sad news followed in 2000, when Yates died of a heroin overdose.)

INXS formed in Australia from the nucleus of the Farriss brothers—Andrew, Jon, and Tim—but the addition of the charismatic Hutchence laid the foundation for the band's success. A wedding of funk grooves to rock guitar, their sound soon took INXS from their Sydney roots to a greater world audience. Hutchence was young and good-looking, with a stage presence that earned him comparisons to

ESSENTIAL LISTENING
The Greatest Hits
Kick

1960–1997

"Disappear"

Jim Morrison and Mick Jagger. The emergence of MTV as a driving force in the music industry couldn't have come at a better time for INXS, with their dynamic pop tunes augmented by the video-ready Hutchence at the fore.

Between 1983 and 1987 INXS enjoyed four hit LPs that encompassed success in the U.S., the U.K., and, naturally, Australia. They produced insistent, unforgettable hits such as "What You Need," "Original Sin," "Need You Tonight," "New Sensation," and "Never Tear Us Apart." Hutchence developed into a forceful singer and basked in the luxury and adulation of finding himself transformed into an international star. He dated beautiful women and posed for the covers of countless magazines. The world was at his feet.

The nineties saw INXS unable to sustain its commercial momentum. A 1992 release topped the British charts and hit the Top 20 in the U.S., but another album the next year failed to break the Top 50. INXS still enjoyed a devoted hard-core fan base, however, and continued to tour successfully.

Hutchence, meanwhile, maintained an undiminished level of celebrity. The camera loved him, and his glamorous international lifestyle made perfect material for selling papers and magazines. Beneath the veneer, though, things started to go wrong for Michael. In 1992 he was in Copenhagen with model Helena Christiansen when he scuffled with a taxi driver and struck his head against a curb. After a period of neglecting his injury, Michael finally went to a doctor. The news was grim: his head injury had greatly diminished his senses of smell and taste, and they would never return. For a passionate sensualist such as Michael, this was devastating news.

Associates say that in the aftermath of this setback, Michael became increasingly depressed and irritable, resorting to Prozac in an attempt to gain emotional equilibrium. He began dating Paula Yates, the wife of British singer and Live Aid organizer Bob Geldof. The paparazzi had a field day. Geldof filed for divorce, and a custody battle over his and Yates's three daughters began. It was a messy situation exacerbated by media pressure and scrutiny—much of it landing in favor of Geldof, often called "Saint Bob" in Britain for his efforts on behalf of famine relief in the mid-eighties. The split between Geldof and Yates was acrimonious, and Hutchence was caught in the middle.

Michael's life was brightened in 1996 by the birth of a daughter with Yates named Heavenly Hiraani Tigerlily, and he optimistically made plans for a solo project. Still, his depression deepened after a 1997 release was largely ignored by the public, and the custody battle with Geldof dragged on. By November of that year INXS returned home to Australia for the final leg of their twentieth anniversary tour. In Sydney on November 21, Michael rehearsed with the band and had dinner with family members. Those who saw him that night reported he was in good spirits, but later in the evening he learned that his wife and daughter would be unable to join him in Sydney for the holidays because of the interminable custody battle with Geldof. He entertained friends in his room at the Ritz-Carlton Hotel until almost five in the morning, talking about the pain and difficulty of his family situation.

The next morning Michael failed to report for a scheduled performance at a Sydney radio station. Around noon a hotel maid entered his room and discovered him naked and hanging from a leather belt. His death was a shock, and his well-attended funeral was broadcast live on Australian TV. Whether Michael Hutchence died of suicide or autoerotic asphyxiation remains a controversial mystery to many, although early the next year a coroner's report concluded that he had killed himself after ingesting alcohol and drugs. In a tragic postscript, Paula Yates died in 2000 from an overdose of heroin. By the end of that year custody of her and Hutchence's daughter was legally granted to Bob Geldof.

> **Tribute to a Friend**
> "He was no tragic figure. He was like oxygen. The room was a dizzier place for him being in it . . . I know he thought suicide was dumb, he didn't buy into it at all. I had conversations with him about Kurt Cobain, saying how sad is that, that Kurt Cobain is gone from the world, and he was angry about that. I find it hard to imagine that Michael took his own life. It doesn't really fit in with my picture of him."
>
> —Bono

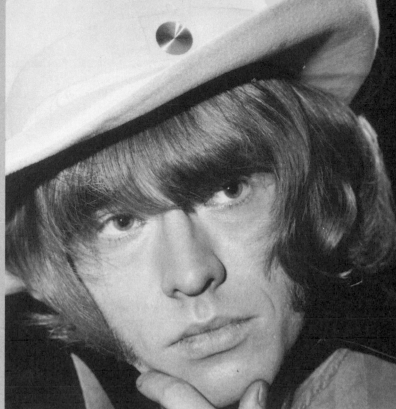

1942–1969

Brian Jones

"It's Just Your 19th Nervous Breakdown"

The Rolling Stones have evolved after four decades into irascible veteran rockers who periodically release new discs and embark on marauding, highly choreographed, and mega-profitable world tours. But time has obscured the early days of the Stones, a time of menace and danger, a world-weary bad trip that nobody embodied in deeper fashion than Brian Jones. He was a dirty pinup who found himself a stranger in his own band, and became the first rock 'n' roll casualty of his generation.

Lewis Brian Hopkins-Jones strayed off the straight and narrow quite early. He was a truant who fathered two illegitimate children while still an adolescent. He was good-looking and cool, and had a natural knack for picking up and playing nearly any instrument he came across. In the early sixties Jones, like scores of other British youth at the time, became entranced with American blues. He dubbed himself Elmo Lewis—oblivious to the fact that he looked nothing like an Elmo—and started playing in a London blues club. Soon he encountered singer Mick Jagger and guitarist Keith Richards—fellow blues enthusiasts—and the three for a time shared a tiny apartment where they wrote songs and honed their technique.

After adding a rhythm section and choosing an appropriately blues-evoking name, the Rolling Stones embraced manager Andrew Loog

Oldham's marketing tactic for the boys: they would be, in essence, the anti-Beatles. They would grow their hair longer, practice their sneers, and generally jab a finger in the establishment's eye. It was a winning strategy, and one that Brian had no trouble acting out—he had an insinuating impudence and blond delinquent beauty that made him a natural early focal point for audiences and the press. He was considered by many at the time to be the leader of the Rolling Stones.

By 1964 the Rolling Stones had charted singles in the U.S. and U.K., and toured America. Their early tracks were covers—Buddy Holly's "Not Fade Away," Bobby Womack's "It's All Over Now," and Willie Dixon's "Little Red Rooster." Jones was the star onstage and in the studio by virtue of his instrumental prowess, but the Stones needed original material if they were going to last in the hypercompetitive music business. Jagger and Richards formed a cadre of two and set about writing an extraordinary string of hit singles that established the Stones as stars of the first magnitude: "(I Can't Get No) Satisfaction," "Get Off My Cloud," "19th Nervous Breakdown," "Mother's Little Helper," "Paint It Black," and "Ruby Tuesday." These songs broke new ground in rock music, with themes of conflict and nihilism laced with sophistication and cynicism.

So where was Brian Jones? Increasingly left out, apparently. He epitomized the air of hustling amorality that lent the Rolling Stones a real sense of danger, but within the group his stature became increasingly diminished. Jones may have been the most authentic bad boy in the group, but Jagger and Richards were the ones doing the heavy lifting on the songwriting factory floor. He began to indulge in drugs and drink, neglecting his duties in the studio. Reports from the mid-sixties have Keith Richards recording multiple tracks on new songs to compensate for Jones's apathetic performance—or complete absence from sessions.

As Jones's star faded, he sank deeper into self-indulgence and substance abuse. In 1967 he suffered a stinging humiliation when Anita Pallenberg, his beautiful model-actress girlfriend, ran off with Keith Richards after becoming fed up with Jones's alleged physical abuse. That same year Jones was busted and convicted of drug possession; his sentence was reduced to a fine and probation after doctors testified that he was suicidally depressed. Jones was ingesting a dangerous combination of cocaine, amphetamines, and hallucinogenics; he became violent and suffered from paranoid delusions. He attempted rehab, but his condition didn't much improve. Jones was being worn down by his constant self-abuse.

The Rolling Stones, always a Darwinian clique, considered Jones a liability and began to think of getting rid of him. They started recording sessions for what would become one of their masterpieces, *Beggar's Banquet*. Richards was still dating Jones's ex-girlfriend, and the group was largely uninterested in whatever musical production the shattered Jones was capable of contributing. Although history has often painted the Stones as callous and selfish, it's worth noting that they kept Jones in the fold during a period in which it might have been tempting to hand him his walking papers.

Perhaps holding out hope for Jones's recovery, they kept mum about his condition in the press and maintained a tenuous equilibrium within the band.

By 1969 Jones had apparently cleaned up his act somewhat. He moved to a house outside London and slowed down the self-flagellating round of drugs that had become his daily fare. But his spirits sank when the Rolling Stones began to plan a tour and took a realistic look at Jones's condition. He was in no shape to withstand the rigors of the road, and in June members of the Stones came to his house to inform him that he was being replaced by guitarist Mick Taylor. Jones released a statement declaring that he was quitting the group because "I no longer see eye to eye with the discs we are cutting"—an ironic claim given that the Stones were recording soulful, innovative blues-rock that Jones at his best would have embraced.

Friends wondered how Brian Jones would fare without the nominal structure afforded by life in the Rolling Stones, and the answer arrived a month later, when, on July 3, he was found dead in his swimming pool. Jones had made enemies during his time at the top, and for a time conspiracy theorists maintained that he had been killed. Nothing concrete ever came from these claims, however, and the coroner ruled that Jones had died of "drowning while under the influence of alcohol and drugs." The Stones played a free concert in London's Hyde Park two days later to an audience of a quarter million; Jagger elegized Jones with a poem by Shelley and released three thousand butterflies. Ironically, most of the butterflies purchased were dead, having been kept sealed in airless cardboard boxes during the show.

And that, effectively, was that. Jones's legacy amounted to a few shining moments of guitar on early Stones tracks, and his dark sitar runs in "Paint It Black" were unique for the day. The Rolling Stones went on for three more decades, first enjoying a run of impossibly great LPs, then settling down into a mixed and sporadic output. Brian Jones was the first major casualty of sixties rock, a talented, narcissistic young man who buckled under the pressures of fame. The one-time leader and founding member of the band had been reduced to a mere footnote.

Thirty Years Later

"He'd let these builders in and they were sort of running his house, y'know, and having fun playing with this stoned-out rock star. I think that maybe somebody held him under the water for a joke and he didn't come up. Murder? No. I think stupidity. I *think.* Weren't there, don't know."

—Keith Richards, in 1999, on Brian Jones's death

Janis Joplin

ESSENTIAL LISTENING
Janis Joplin's Greatest Hits
With Big Brother and the
Holding Company: *Cheap Thrills*
Pearl

"I Got Dem Ol' Kozmic Blues Again Mama!"

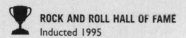
ROCK AND ROLL HALL OF FAME
Inducted 1995

She was a great singer, an exhilarating blues voice with soul and range worthy of consideration alongside the greats of American music. And she was the original rock chick, boozing, drugging, raising hell with a damn-the-consequences attitude. But there was always another dimension to Janis Joplin, some undefinable pain and longing that infused her best vocals, a vulnerability that perhaps found its roots in her origins as an ugly duckling in Port Arthur, Texas, and fueled the drugs-and-alcohol excess that finally killed her at twenty-seven.

Joplin never really belonged in Port Arthur, and by seventeen she had run away from home and started singing in clubs in Houston and Austin. She saved up her money and hit San Francisco, where she was part of an embryonic Bay Area music scene that would solidify in a few years into one of the most vital in the U.S. In 1964, though, Joplin seemed to sense that she was veering too close to her personal edge; she went back to Texas, tried to cut down on her substance abuse, thought about giving up music, and made plans to go to college and get married. In short, she was going straight.

That plan lasted about a year. In 1966 she heard about a promising new band in San Francisco that needed a lead singer. She left her settled-down Texas life and rushed to California, where Big Brother and the Holding Company found themselves with a vocalist. They must have been dumbfounded by their good fortune—Big Brother were a competent if limited boogie-blues band with the prerequisite psychedelic edge of the moment, while Joplin was a whirlwind capable of leaving audiences in a state of slack-jawed awe. She wrung passion, humor, sexuality, and sorrow out of her material—often all in the space of a single verse. Joplin came into her own as singer for Big Brother, and in 1967 they released a debut album and were signed by Albert Grossman, Bob Dylan's manager.

The next year the group released the LP *Cheap Thrills* (a more heartland-friendly version of the record-company-vetoed *Dope, Sex and Cheap Thrills*). It went to #1, and the single "Piece of My Heart" was a Top 20 classic. Joplin metamorphosed into a major celebrity, and she responded in tried-and-true rock-star fashion: she indulged in sex, drugs, and booze on a prodigious scale. A year later she had shed Big Brother and forged out on her own.

Joplin's image was all bawdy bluster. She filled rooms with her outsized personality and her maniacal good-times enthusiasm, and she sported the best and most outrageous hippie finery. She was legendary for being able to drink the boys under the table, and for taking shit from no one. On the road, she drank in local dives while other musicians stayed in the isolated comfort of their hotel or went to more trendy watering holes. Joplin, for all her clamor and roar, seemed to be an extraordinarily sensitive soul who never entirely got over her adolescent isolation and unpopularity. One poignant account has her returning to Port Arthur after she became famous—she envisioned attending her high-school reunion as a conquering hero, and was crushed when she discovered that not even her stardom could grant her acceptance in the small town she professed to repudiate.

Maybe Joplin drank and used drugs to excess in order to ward off her insecurities and self-doubt—she certainly wouldn't be the first, or the last. Maybe she just enjoyed herself too much, and failed to grasp the slippery eel of moderation. Her vices turned into habits, and by the moment of her greatest success she suffered from a bad drinking problem and deepening heroin usage. Joplin was in trouble, and the whirlwind rock'n'roll lifestyle afforded few opportunities for reflection and relaxation. In 1970 she was recording an album with her new Full Tilt Boogie Band and, according to some friends and associates, was enjoying a mood of optimism. But a rebirth was not to be.

On Oct. 4, 1970, Joplin drank at Barney's Beanery in Los Angeles. It was the last time she was seen alive; later she was found dead in her room at the Landmark Hotel in Hollywood. She was found facedown with fresh needle punctures in her arm. The coroner would rule that she had died of an accidental heroin overdose. She was cremated, her ashes spread along the California coast from an airplane.

The record she had been working on was called *Pearl*, after her nickname, and included the track "Buried Alive in the Blues" as an instrumental because Joplin died before recording her vocals. *Pearl* was a #1 hit, as was her single "Me and Bobby McGee"—a classic working of a Kris Kristofferson composition. Joplin died too young, leaving behind memories of her unforgettable personality and a series of classic tracks in a style that few could approach, let alone imitate (although Robert Plant's work on early Led Zeppelin records came close). Hers was a bittersweet legacy of a woman who lived the Kozmic Blues and was eventually done in by them.

A DEADLY ACCIDENT

"Ironically, the reason for Janis Joplin's death was exactly the opposite of the tragedies caused by cut heroin. When an analysis came back from the lab, I found that what the dealer had sold her was almost pure heroin, more than ten times the power of the normal heroin she used. Her system was not prepared for, and could not cope with, the unexpected jolt."

—Thomas M. Noguchi, L.A. coroner

A SENSE OF HISTORY

In August 1970, two months before she died, Joplin helped buy a headstone for the grave of Bessie Smith, an early blues singer who was one of Joplin's most revered influences. Smith had lain in an unmarked grave for more than thirty years after dying of injuries from a car crash in Mississippi.

Terry Kath

"Colour My World"

With a sound that fused horns into gritty rock, Chicago carved a hearty space for themselves on the pastures of seventies American radio with a series of hit singles, Top 10 LPs, and world tours. They would be remembered in the eighties for a more saccharine middle-of-the-road sound that yielded still more chart success at the expense of critical credibility. By that time, though, they steered the ship without the integral influence of guitarist Terry Kath, who died in 1978 following a bizarre gunplay accident.

Chicago emerged in the late sixties from the city that gave it its name; Kath had founded the group as the Big Thing with school buddy Walter Parazaider. A name change to Chicago Transit Authority coincided with the addition of vocalist Peter Cetera, keyboardist Robert Lamm, and the horn section that would enable the group to add an extra dimension of soul and jazz to a vocal-oriented pop-rock style. A series of Top 10 hits followed, including "Does Anybody Really Know What Time It Is?" and "Saturday in the Park." Chicago became one of the most popular acts of the early seventies, recording and touring relentlessly to capitalize on its good fortune.

Terry Kath was an accomplished guitarist whose rock leanings apparently ran counter to his band's direction by the mid-seventies. He was also no stranger to the rock 'n' roll party lifestyle that typified such road-hardened acts

as Chicago. It was at a party in Woodland Hills, California, on January 28, 1978, that Kath became intoxicated on alcohol and was eventually the only remaining guest at the home of road-crew staffer Don Johnson (not the actor). Kath, a gun enthusiast, had apparently brought one from his collection to the party with him, and began twirling it, much to Johnson's consternation. Upon noting Johnson's apprehension, Kath reportedly uttered his last words: "Don't worry, it's not loaded." He then put the gun to his head and pulled the trigger. The gun was indeed loaded, and Kath died from his head wound.

Chicago carried on without Kath, veering hard in the direction of soft-rock balladry. By the time of their commercial renaissance in the eighties, their sound was unrecognizable from the music they'd played a decade before. By the late nineties, Chicago had returned to its musical roots and extensively toured on the back of their seventies hits. Thus the music of founder Terry Kath, plucked from life by a bizarre act of idiotic negligence, returned to the public stage.

ESSENTIAL LISTENING
Chicago IX:—Greatest Hits

An Unlikely Booster
After Terry Kath's death, despondent surviving band members were apparently unsure whether or not to carry on. They were visited after Kath's funeral by Johnny Carson's bandleader, Doc Severinsen, who persuaded them to continue flying the flag of Chicago.

Paul Kossoff

ondon-born Paul Kossoff played one of rock's immortal riffs, still heard daily on classic-rock radio. As guitarist for Free, he was part of one of rock 'n' roll's many short-lived success stories. He then joined the ranks of musicians whose drug use silenced them long before their thirtieth birthday.

Free formed in 1968 from spare parts of Black Cat Bones, Brown Sugar, and the better-known Bluesbreakers. Kossoff's bluesy crunch was well matched with the soulful growling of singer Paul Rodgers. The first two Free albums barely troubled the U.K. charts, but in 1970 the single "All Right Now" was a smash—and rightfully so. One of the most stirring and sinuous interplays of guitar and voice to emerge in rock history, the single hit #2 in the U.K. and #4 in America.

The group failed to follow up on its brief liaison with success, however, and split the next year. Kossoff pursued a side project, then reunited with Free in 1972. The resulting LP, *Free at Last*, was a moderate hit, but troubles arose on the road. Kossoff was a heavy drug abuser, and his body was starting to give out. He missed a tour of Japan, then was unavailable for a string of U.K. dates. The reconstituted Free wasn't long for this world, and Kossoff left to form his own band.

Paul Rodgers and Free's Simon Kirke went on to form Bad Company, a group whose efforts have held up over time more conspicuously than Kossoff's own Back Street Crawler. Kossoff's drug abuse, meanwhile, was overpowering his body. In 1975 Kossoff was on the verge of death for thirty-five minutes in a hospital before he could be resuscitated; the next year he succumbed to a heart attack on a plane flight. He was twenty-five years old. Kossoff's bid for immortality, his playing on "All Right Now," can be heard at least once a day on any of America's classic-rock radio stations.

"Oh, I Wept"

 **ESSENTIAL LISTENING**
Best of Free

Them Hippies Was Tough
"All Right Now" was blocked from becoming a #1 hit in the U.K. by its inability to brush aside a far less muscular piece of music: Mungo Jerry's shuffling "In the Summertime."

Ronnie LANE
"All or Nothing"

London's Ronnie Lane was a bassist and songwriter who played a pivotal part in sixties British rock, then pursued a well-received solo career in the seventies. He had become an elder statesman of sorts when he succumbed after a long battle with debilitating multiple sclerosis.

Lane's first successful band was the Small Faces—so named because they were all less than 5'6" tall. Lane and Steve Marriott were the Small Faces' guiding hands, and they steered the group to a series of British hits. Their only single to make much impact in the U.S. was "Itchycoo Park." Internal divisions in the Small Faces led to Marriott's departure; he would be replaced by singer Rod Stewart and guitarist Ron Wood. Because of the incongruous stature of the new members, the band was forced to rename itself the Faces. The new lineup played harder and dirtier than the Small Faces ever had, and they attained success in the U.S. Eventually Stewart's solo career started to take precedence over his work with the Faces, and in 1973 Ronnie Lane departed to try it alone.

1974 saw the debut of Ronnie Lane's Slim Chance; an ambitious tour followed that included a traveling circus, reportedly shattering Lane's finances. He continued to write and record and, in 1977, released a classic collaboration with the Who's Pete Townshend called *Rough Mix*. The record was possibly Lane's greatest moment, featuring affecting songs such as "Annie" and "April Fool" that perfectly showcased Lane's fragile voice within emotive acoustic folk-rock.

By the late seventies an array of Lane's nagging physical complaints was explained by a diagnosis of multiple sclerosis. He would fight the disease over the course of the next two decades, but his recorded work would greatly diminish as a result of his worsening condition. In 1983 Lane's friends—including Pete Townshend, Eric Clapton, and Jimmy Page—played benefits for multiple sclerosis research on his behalf. Lane would see good years and bad, and last toured in 1990. Finally M.S. killed him in 1997. Lane is usually remembered as a likable and talented man, who plotted his own course within the music world and fought hard against the disease that eventually killed him.

1946–1997

🔊 **ESSENTIAL LISTENING**
With Small Faces: *The Masters*
With Faces: *The Best of Faces: Good Boys When They're Asleep*
With Pete Townshend: *Rough Mix*

1940–1980

John
Lennon

"I Don't Believe in Beatles"

On December 8, 1980, John Lennon was coming home from a recording studio, where he was laying down tracks in a burst of creativity following the November release of his new LP, *Double Fantasy*. A man stepped from the shadows in front of the Dakota building as Lennon got out of his car; he called out Lennon's name and shot him seven times. Lennon died of trauma and blood loss before he reached the hospital. Yoko Ono had been at his side, witnessing her husband's brutal murder. Their son, Sean, was five years old at the time.

John Lennon's death culminated a long trajectory between the brilliant rocker and a disturbed, delusional young fan. Lennon was gunned down by Mark David Chapman, a twenty-five-year-old who had drifted for years amid erratic behavior and psychiatric problems. Chapman, born during the echo of Beatlemania's first wave, had always been an obsessed Beatles devotee. In the years before Lennon's murder, Chapman had become increasingly obsessed by J. D. Salinger's *Catcher in the Rye*—particularly its themes of lost childhood innocence amid the cruelty and hypocrisy of the adult world. Chapman had come to believe that he was *the catcher*, a figure charged with protecting idealism and purity in a world of sellouts, phoniness, and disillusionment. Chapman had come to feel that Lennon—who had been in seclusion from the public eye since 1975, emerging only three weeks before with the release of the LP *Double Fantasy*—had betrayed the utopian ideals of the sixties and become the sort of hypocrite and sellout who needed to be dealt with harshly in order to redeem the world.

Clearly, Chapman was a pathetic figure whose madness inflicted a painful loss on Lennon's family and the world. John Lennon had the tragic distinction of becoming the first prominent casualty of celebrity stalking; Chapman had been in New York for days, getting up his nerve for an attack on Lennon and reportedly also attending a performance by David Bowie in *The Elephant Man* on Broadway. Chapman had been obsessed with Lennon for more than a decade, going so far as to marry an Asian woman to mirror Lennon's partnership with Yoko Ono.

Chapman approached Lennon on the street the day of the murder to autograph a copy of *Double Fantasy*. Lennon obliged, and a photograph survives of Lennon and his eventual murderer, a morbidly fascinating object charged with potent symbolism. The picture shows Lennon giving a moment of his time to a fan who'd dreamed of such a moment all his life, who had projected onto Lennon's image the diseased miasma of his own conflict and turmoil. The arcs of two lives—one lived in the public eye amid decades of adulation, the other spent in obscurity, psychic pain, and starstruck emulation—had finally intersected.

Lennon's musical career hardly needs recounting here. Suffice to say he possessed an incisive and brilliant mind, but he was bogged down by the weight of his legacy five years after the end of the Beatles. Saddled with the baggage of Beatlemania and the sixties, Lennon in the seventies fought to tear away the iconography of his public image. His final songs after emerging from self-imposed seclusion dealt with domestic life, fatherhood, and the insecurities of ordinary middle age. No matter how hard he struggled, though, he remained an icon and a legend—and the object of staggering devotion from a fan base whose emotions toward their idol ran from benign appreciation to murderous rage.

In the two decades since his death, Lennon has remained an icon of peace and idealism. It's a frozen portrait that perhaps obscures his sardonic wit, his sarcasm and skepticism, and his constant artistic search for authenticity and reality. He's become a martyr and a sort of secular saint, but it bears remembering that during his life, John Lennon railed against false idols from the Maharishi Mahesh Yogi to the Beatles themselves. Lennon got into a lot of trouble for his outspokenness and political leftism during his life, but in the end it was the unfortunate outcome of immense celebrity that led to his tragic demise.

ROCK AND ROLL HALL OF FAME
Inducted 1994
Beatles inducted 1988

ESSENTIAL LISTENING
John Lennon/Plastic Ono Band
The John Lennon Collection

1951–1986

ESSENTIAL LISTENING
The Very Best of Thin Lizzy
Jailbreak

Phil
LYNOTT

"Songs for While I'm Away"

Thin Lizzy's brand of testosterone-rich rock made them stars in their native U.K. and earned them lesser albeit respectable American success in the mid-seventies. Their front man, Phil Lynott, was a classic tough guy with a heart of gold who sometimes relented from his drinking-cussing-and-fighting-with-the-boys lyrical approach to pen the occasional ode to his mum or to his true love. Throughout a prolific and turbulent rock 'n' roll career, Lynott fell prey to a deepening drug addiction that led to his death after lapsing into a coma following an overdose.

Lynott was a black Irishman who played in his first professional band while still a teenager. Thin Lizzy was up and running by 1970; an album and subsequent tour the next year occurred with little notice. But by 1973 Lizzy enjoyed its first U.K. hit—"Whisky in the Jar"—which would establish a precedent of insistent power chordage and macho vocals that would essentially see the group through its entire career. In 1976 Thin Lizzy released *Jailbreak*, which scratched the Top 10 in the U.K. and Top 20 in America. The album contained "The Boys Are Back in Town," an homage to male bonding that became Thin Lizzy's signature tune.

Lynott by this time had moved beyond dabbling with hard drugs—particularly heroin—and was developing a habit. He was not alone within the fraternity of Thin Lizzy, a crew that did not epitomize fortitude in the face of temptation. Even while the band was enjoying its greatest success Lynott had begun to suffer health problems, including bouts of hepatitis in 1975 and 1976; the latter episode compelled Thin Lizzy to cancel a series of lucrative American tour appearances.

For a moment Thin Lizzy seemed poised for success on a Zeppelin-like level. Subsequent releases, though, while still charting well back home, failed to improve on *Jailbreak*'s showing. While Lizzy's subsequent albums could be erratic in quality, Lynott still produced material infused with masculine passion and the faint whisper of a poetic heart beating somewhere beneath the bluster. Though his profile had diminished drastically in the U.S. by the early eighties, he was still well known in the U.K. and had earned the respect of late-seventies punks by rocking with them in side bands.

Lynott released solo albums and remained with Thin Lizzy until 1983, when the rot that had set upon the band was too strong to ignore any longer. Lynott formed a group called Grand Slam, and continued to battle his drug problems. In 1985 he was convicted of narcotics possession. The next year his fight ended when he lapsed into a coma after an overdose and died after eight days. His January 4 demise was attributed to "heart failure and pneumonia following septicaemia."

The Little Guy Was Tougher Than He Looked
In 1979, Thin Lizzy's *Black Rose/A Rock Legend* album stalled at #2 in their native U.K. The obstacle that kept mighty Lizzy from the catbird seat? *The Very Best of Leo Sayer.*

Lynyrd Skynyrd

Ronnie Van Zant
1949–1977

Steve Gaines
1949–1977

Allen Collins
1952–1990

"The Smell of Death Surrounds You"

Lynyrd Skynyrd were staunch standard-bearers for the hard-living southern rock tradition inaugurated by the Allman Brothers Band, and after a series of hit records and sold-out tours their star eclipsed even that of their hirsute contemporaries. A plane crash in 1977 tore the heart from these good ol' boys, depriving them of their lead singer and guiding force. More than a decade later another founding member succumbed following a paralyzing accident. Somehow Lynyrd Skynyrd has persevered, overcoming pain and survivor's guilt to endure as a tribute to their fallen comrades. And, incidentally, to rock like hell.

The embryonic Lynyrd Skynyrd emerged from a group of high school buddies in Jacksonville, Florida. They played the local bar circuit for years, developing a tight musical interplay and dense, muscular sound. Lead singer and ringleader Ronnie Van Zant was joined by guitarists Gary Rossington and Allen Collins. Billy Powell on keyboards and Leon Wilkeson on bass were the group's other two permanent members. By 1970 they had settled on their name, a tongue-in-cheek tribute to gym teacher Leonard Skinner, renowned for his intolerance of longhairs such as Van Zant and company.

In 1971, the Allman Brothers Band released their seminal *At Fillmore East*, and American record labels went in search of the next big southern band. Keyboardist and producer Al Kooper found Lynyrd Skynyrd playing in an Atlanta bar and signed them to an MCA subsidiary called Sounds of the South in 1972. The next year saw the release of *Pronounced Leh-Nerd Skin-Nerd* (an obligingly helpful title), a gold record featuring a three-headed guitar attack supplemented by a sessioneer. The LP put Lynyrd Skynyrd on the national map and contained "Free Bird," a Bic-lighter-waving classic tribute to fallen hero Duane Allman and perhaps the group's most enduring classic.

More hit albums followed in the seventies, and after a slot opening up for the Who's *Quadrophenia* tour—Lynyrd Skynyrd were one of the few bands hearty enough to please crowds eager for the Who's particular brand of live thunder—the band became stalwarts of the road. They were hard-living, two-fisted-drinking rowdies. Ronnie Van Zant, in particular, did not neglect his role as rock 'n' roll ruffian, and evinced a famed predilection for the occasional round of fisticuffs after a bout of drinking. Lynyrd Skynyrd were also a solid singles band, producing hits "Sweet Home Alabama" (a shot at Neil Young's Dixie-baiting "Southern Man") and "Saturday Night Special."

The good times came to an abrupt end on October 20, 1977. Lynyrd Skynyrd were traveling from a gig in Greenville, South Carolina, bound for Baton Rouge, when their chartered twin-engine Convair 240 airplane suffered engine trouble and crashed into a Mississippi swamp. Ronnie Van Zant was killed. Also dead was recent addition guitarist Steve Gaines, his sister, backup vocalist Cassie Gaines, and three others. Most other band members sustained serious injuries; drummer Artimis Pyle crawled through the swamp to get help. The plane crash was alarming in its severity, and the survivors had to contend with their own critical injuries in addition to their overwhelming grief. Billy Powell briefed the media daily on the condition of his bandmates while sporting bandages and cuts. Lynyrd Skynyrd had been riding high as one of the top

rock acts in America, but now they were effectively destroyed.

The remaining members—unwilling to tamper with the Skynyrd legacy—regrouped with a female singer in a new incarnation, the Rossington-Collins Band, and released a new LP in 1980. In concert, they performed "Free Bird" as an instrumental tribute to their fallen leader, Ronnie Van Zant. The band dissolved a couple of years later following the death of Allen Collins's wife, and further tragedy struck in 1986, when Collins crashed his car and was paralyzed from the waist down. His girlfriend also died in the accident. In 1990, Collins died of pneumonia in Jacksonville.

Most bands would decide enough was enough in the tragedy department and call it a day. But audiences clamored for more Skynyrd, and the band re-formed in 1987 with original members supplemented by new players, including Ronnie Van Zant's little brother, Johnny, who assumed lead vocal duties. The resuscitated Lynyrd Skynyrd released respectable new material that failed to match the chart success of seventies efforts, but made its real mark on the road. Touring steadily throughout the nineties, they proved capable of filling halls throughout America. In an era when the term "survivor" is applied to anyone who manages to remain standing for a few years or so, Lynyrd Skynyrd has proved amply deserving of the title. Disaster and death have proved incapable of stilling Skynyrd's southern heartbeat.

ESSENTIAL LISTENING
20th Century Masters: The Best of Lynyrd Skynyrd
Pronounced Leh-Nerd Skin-Nerd.

Time for a Marketing Rethink
The 1977 Lynyrd Skynyrd album *Street Survivors* was released just days before the plane crash that temporarily disbanded the group. Its cover depicted members engulfed in flames; MCA withdrew the record and changed the background to somber black. Subsequently the original cover became a morbid collector's item that fetched high prices in used-record stores.

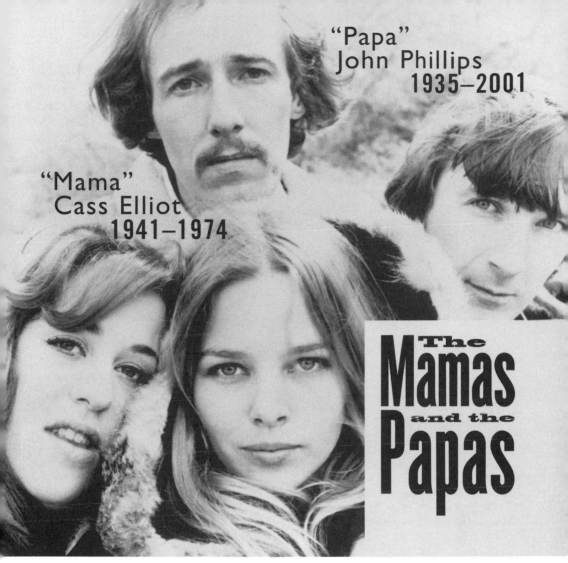

"Papa"
John Phillips
1935–2001

"Mama"
Cass Elliot
1941–1974

The Mamas and the Papas

"Dream a Little Dream of Me"

The Mamas and the Papas, for all their renowned vocal harmonies, were a combustible blend of personalities who endured legendary difficulties getting along with one another that led to multiple lineup changes, breakups, and hard feelings. Their definitive work was produced during a short period in the sixties, and multiple stints on the oldies circuit promoted their perpetually popular greatest hits well into the nineties. Along the way they lost original singer "Mama" Cass Elliot and, more than twenty-five years later, founder "Papa" John Phillips.

John Phillips was a New York folkie who started playing in the late fifties; he enlisted his wife, Michelle, for early bands, and the two quickly assumed the role of proto-hippie ideal couple. John was tall, lanky, and handsome, and Michelle a blonde, waiflike beauty. John Phillips was an ambitious and prolific songwriter in rabid pursuit of musical success through an evolving postfolk, vocal-harmony-based style. By the mid-sixties he had written a parcel of tight, accessible songs, but he had yet to find the right mix of musicians to play them. Enter Mama Cass.

Born Ellen Naomi Cohen in Baltimore, Cass Elliot was a strong singer who had been prominently featured in folk groups since her mid-twenties; with her first husband she formed Cass Elliot and the Big Three, a folk group that transformed into the Mugwumps and followed Bob Dylan's mid-decade electrified lead. Elliot briefly fronted a jazz trio, a testament to the versatility and range of her singing abilities. Success proved elusive for Elliot, however, and by 1965 she was working as a waitress. That same year she accepted an invitation from friends to join them in the Virgin Islands, where they were staying rent-free in exchange for performing at a nightclub. The friends were the New Journeymen—John and Michelle Phillips, along with Denny Doherty—a struggling folk group who had come to the Caribbean to rehearse and rethink their plans for the future. After their self-imposed Caribbean exile, they moved from New York to California and brought Elliot into the fold.

It was a perfect match. The New Journeymen hadn't known it, but they had lacked a crucial fourth vocal part to fit John Phillips's compositions. They became the Mamas and the Papas and released "California Dreamin'" in 1966. Its pop harmonies caught on immediately, and follow-up "Monday Monday" reached #1. The next year's "Words of Love" featured Elliot's vocals and was another hit. By the end of 1967 the Mamas and the Papas had enjoyed six Top 5 singles and become international stars.

The good times weren't meant to last. The Mamas and the Papas' groovy public image prominently featured Michelle Phillips's striking looks, but she was fired briefly in 1966 and expelled for good in 1968—her marriage to the controlling John Phillips was disintegrating, and he refused to remain in the band with her. Added to this strife were love triangles within the Mamas and the Papas that made continuing with an intact lineup an impossible prospect. Henceforth Elliot would be known as Mama Cass, solo artist. John Phillips would embark on a solo career with mixed results.

The initial signs were encouraging for Elliot; a Mamas and Papas track with Mama Cass taking a lead vocal—"Dream a Little Dream of Me"—was a hit a month after the group dissolved. She made her solo stage debut later that year in Las Vegas, but suffered a severe setback after collapsing with a throat hemorrhage and undergoing major surgery. The next year she returned

with a Top 40 single and LP, but by the next year a new release barely scraped the Top 100. The Mamas and the Papas, sensing their moment slipping away for good, attempted a hasty reunion in 1971. The result was a tepid LP, and the band subsequently packed up shop. Phillips went into a period of inactivity, his material comfort ensured by his considerable songwriting royalties.

Mama Cass Elliot remained a well-liked celebrity, known as much for her outgoing public image as for her singing. She was a heavy woman who carried herself with brass and sensuality that made her a natural on the talk-show sofa. Although the Mamas and the Papas' light-harmony sound was no longer in demand, it was easy to imagine improved prospects for Mama Cass's career—the range of her voice enabled her to tackle practically any style. A resurgence was not be, however; on July 29, 1974, Elliot died in London in American singer-songwriter Harry Nilsson's flat. Her death was chalked up to a heart attack she suffered while choking; cruel rumors circulated for decades that Mama Cass had passed away as a result of gluttony. She is better served by remembrance of her talent and her integral part in the short-lived but considerable success story of the Mamas and the Papas.

While ex-wife Michelle went on to a successful acting career, "Papa" John Phillips would re-form the band for oldies tours in the eighties with various members, including his daughter. He also suffered setbacks and trials due to his drug abuse—in 1980, he was arrested by federal narcotics agents for cocaine possession and saw his five-year prison sentence suspended to thirty days after he agreed to lead antidrug lectures. In 1992 he required a liver transplant in Los Angeles. Though his subsequent production of new material was minimal, Phillips settled into an elder-statesman role and spoke eloquently of his days with the Mamas and the Papas. Finally, in 2001, Phillips died of heart failure.

ROCK AND ROLL HALL OF FAME
Inducted 1998

ESSENTIAL LISTENING
California Dreamin': —Greatest Hits

1945–1981

BOB MARLEY

"REDEMPTION SONGS"

Popular music has seen a handful of first-magnitude stars—Elvis, Lennon, Hendrix, Cobain—but no list of this order can be compiled without mention of Robert Nesta Marley. Marley emerged from Jamaica in the seventies as the first and, so far, last global pop star from the Third World. His powerful combination of music, politics, charisma, and undefinable groove made him irresistible to audiences wherever he went. His importance transcended music, his voice spoke for the billions dispossessed by the cruelties of history, and he made a series of albums that stand up against anything in the rock 'n' roll canon. Marley may have just begun to explore the options open to him when, at the peak of his fame, he was diagnosed with terminal cancer. He died well short of his fortieth birthday, leaving an absence that no one has, or probably ever will, come close to filling.

Bob Marley's father was a British army captain from Liverpool named Norval Sinclair Marley. His mother was a Jamaican named Cedella Booker. Marley would grow up not knowing his father, and while still in his teens he left the countryside for Kingston. Life in the city was harsh—Marley took up residence in Trenchtown, one of the most notorious slums in the Third World. When he was seventeen he met powerful record producer Leslie Kong and recorded his first single, "Judge Not." Marley was a precocious talent, and a year later he formed the first incarnation of the Wailers: a vocal group with a ska sound featuring Marley along with Peter Tosh and Bunny Livingston, who would both feature prominently in Marley's subsequent career. Their "Simmer Down" was a big Jamaican hit in 1964.

The Jamaican music business was run by a handful of producers and record-label owners, and artists were routinely shortchanged of their royalties and generally exploited. Therefore, in 1966 the Wailers parted ways and Marley moved to Newark, Delaware, where his mother lived and where he found a factory job. The allure of music was stronger than the prospect of life on an assembly line, however, and Marley soon returned to Jamaica and re-formed the Wailers. In 1969 the group began working with famed eccentric Lee "Scratch" Perry, an all-around musical visionary who encouraged the Wailers to play instruments and expand from a ska singing group into a full-fledged reggae band. The Wailers and Perry produced hits in

Jamaica such as "Trenchtown Rock"—its lyrical references to Jamaica's urban slum were an early sign of where Marley's muse would eventually take him—but the corruption of the music business in their island home ran so deep that even successful artists found themselves enduring a hand-to-mouth existence.

It was also during this time the Wailers underwent a spiritual conversion that is essential to understanding Marley's subsequent life and work. Following a 1966 visit to Jamaica by Ethiopian monarch Haile Selassie, Marley and Tosh converted to the Rastafarian religion. One account has Marley seeing stigmata on the African king's hands, a sight that convinced him of the Rasta belief that Selassie was the messiah of people of African descent, who were in turn the chosen people of God. Rastafarianism is a religion of Third World rebellion, a paradigm shift in which the oppressed people of the world are viewed as its spiritual redeemers. A central practice of Rastafarianism is smoking large amounts of strong marijuana—ganja. Heavy pot smoking as a means to spiritual bliss and enlightenment would be crucial to the Wailers's story from that point forward.

In 1972 Marley's fortunes changed. The Wailers were "discovered" and signed to Island Records. Their global debut, Catch a Fire, was simply stunning. Sensual, pulsing, incendiary, full of great songs—it was a stellar "debut" for a group that had been working together off and on for a decade. The Wailers released a second LP later that year, and their stature grew exponentially when Eric Clapton covered its "I Shot the Sheriff" and turned it into a hit.

The Wailers seemed primed for a long run of success—and they were, although not in their initial form. Island Records favored Marley as

the group's natural star, much to the chagrin of Livingston and, in particular, Peter Tosh. Although the group had been a collaborative effort from the start, Marley's compositions had more universal appeal and his natural charm and good looks led audiences to believe that his band were mere side men. After the second album, both Livingston and Tosh departed. Henceforth the group would be known as Bob Marley and the Wailers.

Marley expanded the band's lineup, adding extra percussion and keyboards along with the I-Threes, three female backup singers. The new Wailers sounded better than ever, rich and emotive and capable of laying a solid foundation for Marley's increasingly polished vocals and captivating songwriting. The band toured the world and became a major act in Britain, charting more than a half-dozen Top 40 hits there. Their global stature by this time was unprecedented for a band that hailed from neither America or Europe. Marley solidified his appeal by crafting achingly beautiful love songs such as "No Woman No Cry," "Is This Love?," and "Waiting in Vain." At the same time he roiled audiences with the politically charged "Exodus," "Stir It Up," and "Concrete Jungle."

If Marley was a major figure outside his home country, he was akin to a deity within it. His stature with the Jamaican citizenry and his clout as an international celebrity made him a powerful player in Jamaican political life. He bought a big house in one of Kingston's oldest and richest districts, where he, his band, and various family members played loud music, smoked *ganja*, and battled endlessly in soccer games on the lawn. His white postcolonial neighbors were reportedly not elated. Marley's high profile must have played a part in the brutal events of December 3, 1976, when seven men invaded his home and began firing shots. Marley was hit, along with his wife and manager. Marley believed that politics were behind the attack, and left for an eighteen-month exile in Miami.

In 1977 Marley underwent surgery to remove a toe after a cancerous growth was detected on it; fans were told that Marley had hurt himself playing soccer. It was an easy lie to believe, for by this time Marley had assumed the aura of invincibility. The next year he headlined the "One Love Peace Concert" in Kingston, a historic moment in Jamaican history. Marley badgered the two leading politicians of the day—Prime Minister Michael Manley and bitter opponent Edward Seaga—into joining him onstage, where Marley clasped their hands above his head and called for national unity. Such was the man's power.

Releases such as *Rastaman Vibration* and *Exodus* were, by this time, charting Top 20 in America. Marley's global domination was complete and well deserved. His songwriting continued to richen, and his vision of Third World rebellion and redemption deepened. But fate intervened during a tour on September 21, 1980, when Marley collapsed while jogging in New York's Central Park. The show that night at Madison Square Garden went as planned, but the remainder of the tour was canceled. Marley soon learned from doctors that he was suffering from cancer.

In May of the next year, his condition deteriorating, Marley flew to his mother's home in Miami. On May 11, he died in Miami's Cedars of Lebanon Hospital. His cancer was incurable and had spread quickly; Marley finally succumbed to lung cancer and a brain tumor. He was buried with full state honors in Jamaica.

CURTIS *Mayfield*

1942–1999

 ESSENTIAL LISTENING
Superfly soundtrack
Beautiful Brother: The Essential Curtis Mayfield
New World Order
With the Impressions: The Very Best of the Impressions

"Keep On Pushing"

With his considerable gifts as a performer augmented by his stellar songwriting and record producing, Curtis Mayfield was one of the most vital figures in American soul and R&B from the late fifties until well into the eighties. A 1990 accident left him confined to a wheelchair and nearly unable to perform, although he rallied in a near-superhuman effort to lay down a final release. His death came quietly, after a decade of struggle, leaving a rich and varied body of work to match nearly any in American popular music.

Born in Chicago, Mayfield's formative performing experience was with the gospel Northern Jubilee Singers. After meeting Jerry Butler, the two formed the R&B group the Impressions in 1957. The Impressions were a powerful vocal ensemble featuring Mayfield's singing, production, and songwriting—much of which incorporated the philosophy of the civil rights movement. Hits included "It's All Right," "Keep On Pushing," "We're a Winner," and "People Get Ready." This was soulful and dynamic music, infused with the uplifting transcendent message of Martin Luther King, Jr.

Mayfield's tenure with the Impressions resulted in a body of work that would have ensured a lofty place in R&B history. In 1970, though, he began a solo career that explored still-new possibilities. Mayfield's first few LPs were solid sellers, and in 1972 he left an indelible mark on America's consciousness with his soundtrack for the blaxploitation movie *Superfly*. The album was a chart-topping success, and even now it's easy to understand why: Mayfield's guitar alternated between wah-wah distortion and insinuating chicken scratch, while his street-life parables were delivered over subtle string arrangements. The lyrics dealt with pushers, drug addicts, and hustlers, and would be an enormous influence on hip-hop more than a decade later.

More hits were to come in the seventies as Mayfield refined his thoughtful lyrical vision and distinctive musical style. By the eighties he had relocated to Atlanta. Although his mainstream success had largely dried up, he remained a presence on the road and—as he always had throughout his career—worked his other artists in a producer's role. Mayfield had a grasp and feel for what worked on record, and he was able to translate his ideas into tracks for Aretha Franklin and Gladys Knight and the Pips.

Early in 1990 Mayfield returned to "Superfly," this time recording the soundtrack to the forgettable film *Return of Superfly*; the resultant LP, *Superfly 1990*, was more relevant, and featured a collaboration with rapper Ice-T, who had acknowledged his musical debt by sampling Mayfield's "Pusherman." Later that year, though, Mayfield suffered a blow from which he would never fully recover. He was performing at an outdoor concert in Park Slope, Brooklyn, on August 14, when winds brought down a lighting rig. The equipment landed on Mayfield and permanently paralyzed him from the neck down.

During the nineties public awareness of Mayfield's legacy blossomed. He was honored in an emotional ceremony at the 1994 Grammy Awards, and that same year a tribute LP of Mayfield covers was released, including contributions from Bruce Springsteen, Elton John, Eric Clapton, and Gladys Knight. Mayfield rallied his energy in 1996 for a final album, the well-received *New World Order*. During the recording he was forced to lie on his back to sing, the only position from which he could marshal enough lung power to deliver his vocals. The fact that he managed to finish an entire LP under conditions of such adversity reveals much about Mayfield's strength of character.

But the effects of quadriplegia continued to erode Mayfield physically, and in 1998 he was forced to have a leg amputated. Finally, on December 26, 1999, Curtis Mayfield died in an Atlanta hospital bed. He marked five decades with his music, and left the memory of an enduring spirit and towering figure in rock and R&B history.

Paul McCartney

1942–1965?

Paul is dead.

"Turn Me On, Dead Man"

Of all the untimely deaths in rock 'n' roll history, none was potentially more shattering and terribly tragic than Paul McCartney's five A.M. demise in a gruesome car accident that decapitated him and left him identifiable only by dental records.

The Beatles' organization, knowing the grief that would erupt once the news was out, quashed the information and set out in frantic search of a Paul look-alike. They found William Campbell, who was immediately touched up with plastic surgery until he could pass for a living, breathing Paul (they missed the scar under his lip, but no one would ever notice).

There were complications—the Beatles would have to stop playing live, for instance. And the cover-up would require decades of diligent maintenance. Of course the surviving Beatles, racked with guilt, began leaving little messages in their songs and on their album sleeves for those who were acute enough to notice them . . .

Sound crazy? It sure does. But in the mid-sixties, Beatles obsessives began poring over LP covers and lyrics in search of clues to prove their thesis: Paul was dead.

But what's stranger is that more and more "clues" began to appear. The harder one looked, the more clues one found. Aided by states of chemical enhancement, some Beatles fans felt as though they were being initiated into a secret circle of knowledge, as though John, George, and Ringo were passing along secret messages about their fallen comrade.

The list of clues is too many to duplicate in detail (myriad books and websites can supply the minutiae of the theory), but consider some high lights that begin in 1965:
•Paul is inside a trunk on the U.S. album *Yesterday and Today*, signifying his new position inside a coffin.

•The cover of 1965's *Rubber Soul* is shot looking up to represent McCartney's vantage point from the grave.
•The sleeve of *Sgt. Pepper's Lonely Hearts Club Band* contains visual clues aplenty. Symbols including open palms, the use of the color black, smashed model cars, and floral funeral arrangements all indicate that Paul is no longer with us.
•Lyrical references to car crashes, losing one's head, five in the morning, leaving, and no longer being with us begin to abound on the band's recorded output.
•The cover of *Abbey Road* features, famously, the Beatles crossing the street in funeral procession. White-dressed John is the preacher, Ringo in his suit is a pallbearer, barefoot Paul is the corpse, and denim-clad George is the gravedigger.
•Turntable reversers across the country claim to find backward messages, including "Turn me on, dead man," and the less subtle "Paul is dead." Some claim George Harrison wails a grievous "Paul, Paul, Paul" at the end of his "While My Guitar Gently Weeps."

So what's the truth? Could it be that Paul McCartney really died in 1965, and that ever since we've lived with the impostor William Campbell?

Well, it *would* explain the first Wings album.

But no, no. Paul McCartney is alive and well. But what about all those clues? The deeper one delves into this morbid iconography, the more one senses a purpose behind it, a distinct feeling that someone on the other side is laughing. So was it all a hoax, a big joke from the Beatles?

We can't say for sure. But the fact remains that they've been amazingly tight-lipped about it ever since.

Paul is dead.

FREDDIE MERCURY

ROCK AND ROLL HALL OF FAME
Queen inducted 2001

"KILLER QUEEN"

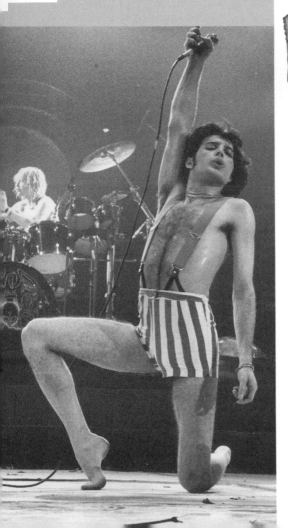

I n the seventies, Queen front man Freddie Mercury seemed to have sprung fully formed from the brow of some decadent, perverse deity—his outrageous stage persona and soaring operatic voice, laid atop squealing sci-fi metal, had to be seen and heard to be believed. Queen ruled the rock world for much of the decade and, when their U.S. success waned, they continued to reign over much of the rest of the globe. Nothing could stop them, it seemed, until Mercury confirmed on his deathbed what he and the band had denied for years—he was suffering from AIDS. Only a few days later, he was dead.

Mercury was born Farrokh Bulsara in colonial Zanzibar, where his father was a government accountant; the younger Bulsara was subsequently sent off to boarding school outside Bombay until his family returned to England when he was seven. He graduated with a degree in graphic art and design and initiated a fashion stall in London's Kensington Market. Soon he was playing with drummer Roger Taylor and guitarist Brian May (the latter beginning to hone his distinctive glam-influenced pop-metal sound). In 1971 the group added bass player John Deacon and dubbed itself Queen. They avoided the rigors of touring while various members pursued college degrees, but the next year they bagged a record deal and began to devote themselves to their music. Bulsara had transformed himself into Freddie Mercury, a shameless stage hog and tongue-in-cheek preening rock god.

Queen built their fortunes gradually, and their third LP, *Sheer Heart Attack,* hit the U.S. Top 20—by then, they were already firmly established in the U.K. Their next release went supernova: *A Night at the Opera* featured the vocal extravaganza "Bohemian Rhapsody." The song was a revelation at six minutes of length, with Mercury's intricate layered vocals invoking all sorts of aural exotica until a crazed Brian May guitar solo brought the whole thing tumbling down into an orgasmic rush. It was a Top 10 hit in the U.S. and topped the British charts. Queen were certified stars.

Mercury wasted no time playing the part of globe-straddling rock 'n' roll god; he indulged in a hearty assortment of vices and a full glass of decadence mixed with a shot of hedonism (one biographer reports that Mercury's cocaine and vodka bills at one point reached a thousand pounds a week). At his epic parties, which featured the prerequisite seventies blizzard of cocaine, young boys were reportedly carried out on giant serving platters in a self-conscious parody of Roman imperial vice. Which brings up the interesting point of Mercury's homosexuality; although Mercury himself took no great pains to hide it, a vast portion of his young teenaged male record-buying public was oblivious to their hero's sexual orientation. Mercury was camp and flash, and in retrospect he was the great gay rock star of the seventies (with apologies to Elton John). At the time, there were questions: Is he or isn't he? It was, it's fair to say, a less perceptive time.

The decade belonged to Queen. The group scored hits with compositions from each band member, and their series of LPs in these years yielded an assortment of hit singles that remain staggering in their vigor and variety. The hits kept coming: "You're My Best Friend," "Somebody to Love" "We Are the Champions"/"We Will Rock You." The stakes were raised even higher with the 1980 release of *The Game,* which contained the ubiquitous #1s "Crazy Little Thing Called Love," and "Another One Bites the Dust." Queen were a stadium-filling monster, with Mercury playing to vast, adoring crowds. He began to sport a butch mustache-and-tank-top look in place of his previous flamboyant outfits. The world was Freddie Mercury's, and, by most accounts, he took full advantage of his opportunities for excess and indulgence. All the while, he maintained a knowing, nudge-and-a-wink charm that endeared him to both the fans who *got it* and those who didn't.

American chart success dried up for Queen in the eighties, but they responded by pretending not to notice. Their LPs continued to hit the Top 10 in their native England, and they filled soccer stadiums pretty much everywhere else in the world they chose to play. In 1985 they played Live Aid at Wembley Stadium (famine-relief activist Bob Geldof said it was the "perfect stage for Freddie. He could ponce about in front of the whole world"). The next year Queen played its 658th and final concert. In the years to come, Mercury's public appearances would become less frequent, and he would seem increasingly sick and gaunt. Eventually rumors that he was suffering from AIDS surfaced, followed by a slew of tabloid allegations. Mercury and the band denied the reports.

But behind their edifice of denial Mercury was physically ailing. He did have AIDS, although after informing the group he swore them to secrecy. In 1991, Queen's *Innuendo* LP topped the British charts upon its release. The lyrics dealt opaquely with Mercury's condition, and footage from the sessions reveals that he was thin and pale, and that finishing the project had required enormous will and stamina from the suffering vocalist. In November he released a statement confirming the AIDS rumors; two days later he died quietly in his home.

Some have called it the big disease with the little name, and there's no doubt that AIDS had felled a talent and personality of legendary proportions. The following years the surviving Queen members staged a concert that featured guest vocalists including David Bowie, Elton John, Annie Lennox, Mercury influence Liza Minnelli, and Axl Rose. The show was broadcast to an audience of a billion, and cemented Freddie Mercury's place as a beloved figure in rock history. There was, simply, no one remotely like him.

ESSENTIAL LISTENING
Queen: *Greatest Hits*
A Night at the Opera
The Game

Keith Moon

"Can You See the Real Me?"

was never one to shirk his duties as professional lunatic in a massively successful rock 'n' roll band. Nor was he exempt from the risks associated with the job—partially deafening his guitarist after setting off an explosion in his drum kit; facing down the massive bills after he demolished hotel rooms; and, finally, succumbing to the toll on his body from years of gargantuan drink-and-drug abuse. Keith Moon took on the heady chores of being the Who's resident madman, and it did him in. Although he seemed ready to slow down a bit at the end of his life—after treating his tenure with the band as a pretense for one extended debauch—he paid the ultimate price for his legendary excesses, and died at thirty-one.

Moon was a strange, manic, over-the-top character. He was also an excellent drummer, and his playing on the Who's varied output evoked a spirit of restlessness and chaos wedded to exuberance and fervor. Live, he was a blur of arms and legs, usually topped off by a lunatic's grin. The Who were one of the biggest bands of their day, and their success afforded Moon ample opportunities to indulge his propensities for booze, drugs, and enthusiastically bizarre behavior.

Cataloguing his outrages entails opening one's mind to the many-faceted possibilities of rock-star excess. In 1967 Moon set off a gunpowder blast in his drums for the finale of a performance on *The Smothers Brothers Comedy Hour*. The explosion singed guitarist Pete Townshend's hair and precipitated ear damage that would leave him nearly deaf in middle age. Moon himself was cut on the leg by shrapnel from a broken cymbal. To polish off a birthday party the next year that was already brimming with monumental merrymaking, he drove a Lincoln into a Holiday Inn swimming

ESSENTIAL LISTENING
My Generation: The Very Best of the Who
Who's Next
Quadrophenia

Strange Irony
While posing for the cover of *Who Are You*, the band's final recording with Moon, Keith's bloated belly was sending off a very non-rock-star message to the camera. To hide his paunch, they had him sit backward in the nearest available chair. By odd coincidence it bore a paint-stenciled message: *Not to Be Taken Away.*

 THEY SAID IT

"I used to look at Keith and think, 'This guy is gonna die,' and I was afraid for him. And I still struggle with, as I think Roger does, our complicity in that. It was *useful* for us to have this crazy man in the band. It got us publicity."

—Pete Townshend

"He never seemed able to get offstage. He always had to be Keith Moon. He was playing the part of Keith Moon because he couldn't remember what it was like to be normal. The only time he was normal was before two in the afternoon. After two he became his alter ego."

—John Entwistle

pool. In 1972 Moon appeared as a nun in a Frank Zappa movie. The next year he collapsed onstage at the Cow Palace in San Francisco after ingesting a horse tranquilizer (a fan from the audience was enlisted to finish off the concert in place of the incapacitated Moon). Feeling the need to break out from the Who, in 1975 he released a solo LP, *Two Sides of the Moon*, that is remembered most for its stunning awfulness. Filled with a yen for redecorating the next year, he paid nine New York cabdrivers a hundred dollars each to block a street below his hotel room so he could toss the furniture out into the street without injuring passersby.

Moon's legend grew in proportion to his latest fiendish stunt, and his ongoing lunacy was fueled by a staggering portion of booze and drugs. When the group convened in 1978 to record *Who Are You*, Townshend, Daltrey, and Entwistle were alarmed by their friend's deterioration. Moon was bloated and unhealthy, and his playing was suffering as a result. Later that year he tried to contain his drinking by taking the prescription drug Heminevrin, but this proved to be his undoing on September 8, when his girlfriend discovered him dead in bed in their flat. The night before, they had attended the premiere of *The Buddy Holly Story*, and Moon had stunned her by opting for an early exit instead of his usual antics. That night, while she slept, he overdosed on the pills that were supposed to help wean him from liquor. The Who would eventually continue on, but even they were willing to admit that they would never be the same band without him. Keith Moon's legendary appetites and acts had turned him into one of rock's greatest casualties.

Jim Morrison

"Break on Through to the Other Side"

Wild Times in the Afterlife

Morrison had been disowned by his family by the time of his death, so he was buried in at Père-Lachaise cemetery in Paris—also home to the remains of Chopin, Balzac, Oscar Wilde, and Edith Piaf. His headstone read "*Kata ton daimona eay toy*," a Greek translation of "True to his own spirit." Over the years his grave was perpetually painted with graffiti and strewn with appropriate gifts to Morrison—booze, cigarettes, girls' underwear, the sort of things he would have enjoyed. In 1990 the headstone was stolen by an overzealous fan, and in 1993 hundreds flocked to the cemetery for what would have been Morrison's fiftieth birthday.

ROCK AND ROLL HALL OF FAME
The Doors inducted 1993

There are those who would maintain Jim Morrison was a Dionysian genius, an era-defining shaman, a psychedelic seer, and an immortal beauty. Those intent on tearing down his legend assert he was a rambling drunk, a mediocre poet, and a bloated burnout. There is truth in each opinion, for Jim Morrison was both one of rock's most influential stars and one of its greatest casualties. Morrison took the raw material of Elvis Presley's charismatic swagger and wedded it to Bob Dylan's love of poetry and contempt for convention. To the mix he added his own brand of malevolence and brooding vision. Elvis was a rocker who wanted the world to love him, and the Beatles were stars whose public image enveloped their millions of fans like a warm embrace. Morrison was different: he sought to disturb and inflame, he stoked the flames of the id and reveled in the results.

Morrison was a child from a military family who was turned loose in southern California during a time when America's conventions and deepest assumptions came under tumultuous assault. He seized the moment and became a new kind of rock star—sinister and primal, yet literate and poetic, with a charisma that encouraged his fans to regard him as a mythic figure. Morrison then rode his fame and vision straight down into a miasma of drink and drugs, the mad Lizard King, fat and shopworn by the time of his death in Paris. Some speculated that the intensity of Morrison's muse and the electric high-wire act he played out on the world's stage overwhelmed him.

Those people are probably right.

Then there is the matter of those who believe Morrison never died, that he sensed the lightning bolt a moment before it was due to strike, that he saved his own skin by faking his demise and escaping the public eye before he succumbed to madness and death.

Those people are probably wrong.

The Doors started in 1965, when Morrison recited one of his poems, "Moonlight Drive," to film school acquaintance Ray Manzarek. Ray played keyboards and was suitably impressed with the poem's evocative imagery, and he suggested they start a band together. They added a guitarist named Robby Kreiger, whose style was steeped in jazz and blues rather than standard rock riffage. With the addition of drummer John Densmore the lineup was set. Jim named the group after Aldous Huxley's *The Doors of Perception*; the band played several months of gigs, then landed a record deal and entered the studio.

To say that the Doors peaked early would be an understatement. Their first LP, daringly titled *The Doors*, was inarguably their only great album. The music was strange and dramatic, full of thrumming organs and sparse guitar parts. Atop it all was Jim Morrison crooning about death, altered states of being, carnality, and the Oedipus complex. It was 1967, and bands from southern California weren't supposed to sound like this—dark, sinister, brooding. From this astounding debut, a catchy ditty called "Light My Fire" went to #1. Another cut, "The End"—the tune that precipitated the end of their residency at L.A.'s famed Whisky-A-Go-Go—broke unprecedented ground in rock music via a spoken-word section in which Morrison assumed the character of a psychopath murdering his family and screaming his desire to have intercourse with his mother.

It was heady stuff, and Morrison became a star overnight. For a time he enjoyed a twisted sort of schizoid fame: He was featured in teen magazines as a pinup idol, while at the same time adults reckoned with the malignant poetry of his lyrics and sneering, haughty image. In 1968 the Doors enjoyed a second #1 hit with "Hello, I Love You." But by then the rot had already set in. Morrison was a heavy drug user and drinker, and while the Doors's subsequent albums featured classic tracks, they were also characterized by filler and a counterweight of mediocre material. While the band began a creative decline, the strange days were by no means over.

Morrison at his best was the epitome of cool, wild-eyed with flowing hair, dressed in skintight leather pants and conducting himself generally like an evil Elvis sprung whole from the mustiest subbasement of the American unconscious. He envisioned his concerts as mass rituals in which he assumed the role of a transgressive shaman; he exhorted his audiences to abandon their inhibitions, goading and taunting everyone and everything. He proclaimed himself the Lizard King, muttering on record *"I can do anything!"* (hey, it sounded heavy at the time). In short, he went a little crazy, and he took rock music into the realms of myth and poetry.

The dark side of his incendiary behavior dogged his days with the Doors. In 1967 he was arrested at a show in New Haven after berating the police onstage. His most damaging arrest came in 1969 in Miami, where he was charged with "lewd and lascivious behavior in public by exposing his private parts and by simulating masturbation and oral copulation." A month after the arrest Morrison was busted by the FBI in L.A. and charged with interstate flight and trying to skip out on his legal problems in Miami. Most of the Miami charges against him were eventually dropped for lack of evidence, but only after lengthy court proceedings that kept the Doors off the road and wore down his endurance. His drinking continued, he began to put on weight, and his psyche began to sag under the weight of persecution over his challenges to authority and the established order. That same year the band released a Top 10 LP, *The Soft Parade*, but it was a lethargic and overproduced affair.

Yet another arrest followed in November 1969, when a drunken Morrison was charged after a run-in with a flight attendant—a potentially serious matter, because it involved U.S. federal aviation law. During a concert early the next year, he asked the audience if they'd like to have a look at his genitals; to prevent him from following through on this generous offer, the hall staff switched off the power. In October, Morrison received a harsh blow when he was finally convicted of charges in Miami stemming from his public-exposure incident and sentenced to eight months' hard labor. Although he remained free pending appeal, he was looking at the sobering prospect of doing hard time.

Morrison's life had spiraled out of control. His vices had become habits, and his bloated, bearded appearance bore little resemblance to the slim, mad Lizard King. He recorded a final LP in 1971 with the Doors, *L.A. Woman*, then announced he was taking time off from the group. In early 1971 he moved to Paris to concentrate on writing poetry—he had already gone into a studio the November before, on his twenty-seventh birthday, and recorded poetic readings that careened between hallucinatory imagery and drunken rambling. Morrison's fresh start and hoped-for creative renaissance was not to be. On July 3, 1971, he was found dead in his bathtub in Paris. His death was chalked up to a "heart attack induced by respiratory problems."

Jim Morrison had shone brightly and burned out quickly. But in death his story turned into myth, and the Doors enjoyed several waves of popular resurgence. The first came in 1980 with the Danny Sugerman–Jerry Hopkins biography *No One Here Gets Out Alive*. Record sales exploded, and Morrison was back on the cover of *Rolling Stone* with the tag line "He's Hot, He's Sexy, He's Dead." In 1991 the Oliver Stone film *The Doors*, with Val Kilmer playing Morrison, sparked another wave of record sales and public interest in him and the band. Several greatest-hits packages became perennial sellers, and the remaining members of the band regrouped occasionally to play with superstar singers taking Morrison's place at the microphone. There were continued rumors that he hadn't died, that he had faked his death to avoid his prison sentence and the heavy weight of his fame. He had been buried quickly, with few witnesses viewing his corpse. To this day there are those who insist that Jim Morrison is alive somewhere, laughing at us all. It's unlikely that anyone could have maintained the illusion of his death in the face of such posthumous fame (and royalties), but the mystery is appropriate to a figure of his perversity. If his death was a fake and a joke, it was a damned good one.

ESSENTIAL LISTENING
The Doors Greatest Hits
The Doors

Rick Nelson

 ROCK AND ROLL HALL OF FAME
Inducted 1987

"Travelin' Man"

In the late fifties and early sixties, Ricky Nelson enjoyed the advantageous position of releasing records which he also performed on one of America's most popular weekly TV shows. He was one of the biggest teen idols of his time. A major letdown occurred later, when Ricky became "Rick" and released challenging adult music. Although he never rescaled the heights of his early success, Rick Nelson continued to write and perform, and to contend uneasily with his past. His death in a plane crash was tainted with unfounded allegations of drug abuse, but in the fifteen years since he has assumed a respected place in the history of rock 'n' roll—a genuine accomplishment, considering the pitfalls that lay in wait for the unsuspecting teen star grown up.

Nelson ruled the fifties when he was little more than ten years old. *The Adventures of Ozzie and Harriet,* featuring Rick with his parents and brother, began as a radio series and moved to television in 1952. It was a hit, an iconic representation of

American family life, and little Ricky was an audience favorite. In 1957 he started singing on the show, and his built-in popularity made him a young rock star. He enjoyed more than a dozen Top 10 hits and million sellers. "Poor Little Fool" and "Travelin' Man" topped the charts. By the time *Ozzie and Harriet* went off the air in 1966, Nelson was married with children, and his days as a teen idol were behind him.

Nelson suffered the perceived credibility deficit suffered by many fifties stars heading into the sixties, and his problems were compounded by the double whammy of his outgrown teen-idol status. It was a creative straitjacket, and for a time Nelson plunged into film work to supplement his increasingly lackluster recording career. He turned a corner musically in the late sixties, when he began to record tracks by Bob Dylan, Hank Williams, and Willie Nelson. He formed the Stone Canyon Band and veered in the direction of L.A.'s emerging country-rock scene. He had a hard time getting his audiences to go along for the ride. Many times they shouted for the old fifties hits, for which Nelson had little enthusiasm. He was booed at a rock 'n' roll revival show in New York when he took the stage with long hair and a country sound. The experience moved him to compose "Garden Party," which was a creative triumph and a Top 10 record in 1972.

It was to be a final high-water mark. He bounced from label to label, releasing LPs that failed to find an audience. He responded by hitting the road, playing more than two hundred shows a year into the early eighties. He mixed new material with old, but resolutely refused to become a nostalgia act like so many of his contemporaries—even though such a move surely would have netted him greater proceeds. Nelson was on tour in 1985 when, on December 31, a plane chartered to take him and his band to a show in Dallas caught fire and crashed; Nelson perished along with his fiancée, his sound engineer, and his backing band. There were rumors that the fire had started because passengers were freebasing cocaine in the cabin—allegations that were refuted by a National Transportation Safety Board Investigation. After his passing, he was remembered with fondness by his fellow artists, and no less a luminary than Bob Dylan played Nelson's "Lonesome Town" in concerts the following year.

 ESSENTIAL LISTENING
Ricky Nelson Volume 1 and Volume 2
Best of Ricky Nelson
Bright Lights and Country Music/Country Fever

No Lightweight
While trying to break away from his pinup past by transforming into a country rocker, Rick Nelson attracted stellar company for his efforts. His records and bands included Roger McGuinn and former and future members of the Eagles, Little Feat, Buck Owens's band, the Desert Rose Band, and the New Riders of the Purple Sage.

"I'll Be Your Mirror"

nico 1938–1988

Nico was the chanteuse of the Velvet Underground's underworld of the soul, her cold Teutonic vox lending an unexpected turn to a handful of Lou Reed classics during her brief semi-membership in the band. She went on to explore the prosaic terrain of suicide, pain, and depression in her own solo career. Not a "true" musician, Nico did possess an unmistakable voice that was an acquired taste. Although she didn't sing Reed's classic "Heroin," she was no stranger to the stuff, suffering decades of addiction before dying after a bicycle accident in Spain.

Born Christa Päffgen in Germany, Nico was a fashion model when she cut a single for Rolling Stones' manager Andrew Loog Oldham. Her orbit soon intersected with that of Andy Warhol's Factory, and the pop artist introduced her to the Velvet Underground's Lou Reed and John Cale. She appeared on a few cuts of the band's 1967 debut, *The Velvet Underground and Nico,* but was gone by the next year. Always one to make fortuitous connections, Nico had a song written about her by Bob Dylan ("I'll Keep It with Mine"), and for her solo debut, *Chelsea Girl,* in 1968 she recorded some tracks by a then-unknown sixteen-year-old Jackson Browne. She also enjoyed a brief relationship with Jim Morrison, and performed "The End" as a concert staple for years.

Nico's solo years were patchy and seldom made for easy listening. She made harrowing, arty, anticommercial records that appealed to only the most devoted cult audience. Heroin addiction dogged her adult life, and she spoke of privations and abuses suffered during her childhood in postwar Germany. She had a patron of sorts in John Cale, who faithfully returned to the mixing desk time and again to produce her records—including her final release, *Camera Obscura.* She had reportedly managed to control her addiction to methadone when she had a bicycle accident in 1988 while on holiday in Ibiza, Spain; a taxi driver found her by the road and took her to a hospital, where she was misdiagnosed as suffering from sunstroke. She was dead a day later from a cerebral hemorrhage.

ESSENTIAL LISTENING
The Velvet Underground and Nico
The Classic Years
Chelsea Girl

Harry Nilsson

He was known as a gifted songwriter, singer, and musician—and also as John Lennon's drinking buddy during the latter's L.A. debauch of the mid-seventies. For a time earlier in that decade, Nilsson's voice and song craft clicked with mass audiences. After a lengthy period spent away from making music, he was readying a set of new songs when he was felled by heart disease.

Nilsson was toiling nights at a bank in Van Nuys in the mid-sixties, all the while spending his days writing songs and trying to break into the music business. He got a foot in the door in 1961, when he sold three of his songs to famed producer Phil Spector. After the Monkees picked up Nilsson's "Cuddly Toy," his stock rose and he signed to RCA Records. A couple of subsequent solo releases could be found nowhere on the charts, but his fine song craft earned him a cult following and the admiration of his peers. After the release of *The Pandemonium Shadow Show*, Nilsson received a call from John Lennon expressing the Beatle's fondness for the LP.

In 1969 Nilsson's profile rose when Three Dog Night covered his tune "One," earning a #5 hit. Nilsson inaugurated a run of successes that included "Everybody's Talkin'," the theme from the film *Midnight Cowboy* and one of the most popular songs of 1969. Two years later he released *Nilsson Schmilsson,* which was a Top 10 hit and spawned #1 single "Without You," a Badfinger cover. "Schmilsson" was a sort of cheesy doppelgänger for Nilsson, and in 1972 he exploited the concept further on *Son of Schmilsson*, which reached the Top 20. Nilsson would never again match this chart success, but it certainly was a respectable run.

Nilsson became notorious in the mid-seventies, when he was often seen with John Lennon; the latter was temporarily separated from wife Yoko Ono and abdicated to L.A. for a Herculean bout of dissolute behavior. Nilsson himself reportedly enjoyed more than a glass of wine at bedtime, and he and Lennon bent elbows together on more than one occasion. Nilsson continued to record, but by the early eighties he had stepped away from music to start a family and concentrate on business concerns. He made a record in 1988 called *A Touch More Schmilsson in the Night*, which contained covers and old material. A heart attack in 1993 motivated Nilsson to begin writing again, and he had just finished his first new batch of songs in thirteen years when he fell ill while getting into his car on the way to a Jimmy Webb show in January 1994. He was dead of heart disease at 52. He left behind a wife and seven children, along with a small but devoted fan base.

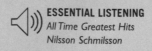

ESSENTIAL LISTENING
All Time Greatest Hits
Nilsson Schmilsson

An Affectionate Farewell
A 1995 tribute release called *For the Love of Harry (Everybody Sings Nilsson)* featured contributions from Brian Wilson, Aimee Mann, Ringo Starr, Stevie Nicks, Randy Newman, and many others.

"Without You"

NOTORIOUS B.I.G.
1972–1997

ESSENTIAL LISTENING
Life After Death
Ready to Die

'BIG POPPA"

Brooklyn's own Christopher Wallace lived large on the streets; in his teens he was reportedly the proud operator of a thriving crack-dealing franchise. He also lived large at the supper table, tipping the scales clean over by loading almost three hundred pounds onto his 6'3" frame. Calling himself Biggie Smalls, he went into rapping, which, one might have hoped, would have afforded him a longer life span than drug dealing. Tragically, that notion proved unfounded.

Notorious B.I.G. rapped on the Mary J. Blige hit single "What's the 411?" He subsequently hooked up with Sean "Puffy" Combs's Bad Boy empire. In 1994 his debut, *Ready to Die*—prophetic title and all—was one of the most vital hip-hop releases of the decade, and spawned the hit "One More Chance." Biggie imparted his raps with the harsh blood and degradation of his life on the streets, leavened with a sense of weariness and fatalism. His music was dark and moving, and he quickly became one of the most successful stars in hip-hop.

Unfortunately, just as Biggie's musical profile grew, so did his embroilment in the nineties West Coast–East Coast hip-hop feud. Biggie in particular was enemies with rap star Tupac Shakur, who inflamed the ill will between the two men by claiming on record that he'd slept with Biggie's wife. The rhetoric between the Bad Boy and Death Row Records camps grew increasingly venomous, and suspicions that the rivalry was mere publicity seeking or harmless posturing were erased when Shakur was murdered in Las Vegas on September 13, 1996. Biggie was preparing his second Notorious B.I.G. release at the time, and he and Combs vehemently denied any involvement in Shakur's brutal shooting.

The rap world was surrounded with uncertainty and a sense of lethal violence boiling under the surface in those months, and on March 9, 1997, dire fears came true. Biggie Smalls was returning to his Los Angeles hotel following a Soul Train Awards party; another car pulled up alongside his, a gunman opened fire, and Biggie was killed instantly. His second release, *Life After Death*, debuted at #1 three weeks later. As of this writing, Biggie's and Tupac's killers have yet to be found.

PHIL OCHS

1940–1976

Let the Buyer Beware

By 1971 the writing was on the wall for the folk protest movement. Ochs responded by donning gold lamé, fronting a band of L.A. session players, and recording the live *Gunfight at Carnegie Hall*. He performed his own greatest hits, along with Elvis and Buddy Holly songs, and a rendition of Merle Haggard's "Okie from Muskogee." The LP, with a mix that left in the sound of the audience booing, was released only in Canada.

"THERE BUT FOR FORTUNE"

Phil Ochs was part of an America that exists only in the new millennium's memory; a folksinging protest troubadour and voice of the angry Left, his musical legacy has to be understood in the context of the history of his times. The strange downward spiral that led to his suicide in 1976, though, breaks from history's conventional mold of rock-styled drugging and drinking, and reflects the often-tragic touch of fate.

Though he was born in Texas, Ochs's family moved to New York when he was still a small child. After a Virginia military school and a college stint in Ohio studying journalism, Ochs returned to New York in 1961. Ochs started writing songs during a stay in jail for vagrancy, and soon was part of the same Greenwich Village leftist folk scene as Bob Dylan. In 1964, his tunes "I Ain't Marchin' " and "Draft Dodger Rag" captured the mounting anti–Vietnam War sentiment among American youth. For his troubles Ochs was banned from radio and TV in the home of the brave.

Ochs was active in protest movements and antiestablishment politics, remaining for a time locked into the folksinging mode that Bob Dylan cast aside in favor of rock's broader palette. His own coffers were enhanced by the Top 50 success of Joan Baez's version of his "There But for Fortune" in 1965. In 1968, years after Dylan plugged in and rocked out, Ochs began to mix electric tunes with acoustic folk numbers on his records. By and large, the general public was uninterested.

When the seventies dawned, America was nagged by the sense that the optimism of the sixties was about to give way to something darker and more cynical. Ochs was no different, and his mind-set gave way to depression as he looked back on the protest movement he'd staked his life and career upon, and that was now seeming to dissolve. The Left was still breathing, but it was becoming apparent that the utopian vision of the sixties was going to remain an illusory ideal. And the folk scene was all but dead.

In 1973, Ochs's fortunes took a turn for the tragic. While traveling in Africa he was mysteriously assaulted and almost killed. Ochs's assailant nearly strangled the singer to death, and in the process dealt him perhaps a harsher blow: Ochs's vocal cords were permanently damaged, and his voice was never to be the same.

Ochs occasionally continued to perform, but his voice was no longer up to the task. He drank heavily and plunged into an increasingly dark depression. One account has him changing his name to John Butler Train and no longer answering to the name Phil Ochs. By late 1975 he was staying with his sister in Queens; the next April he would hang himself there.

It didn't look as though Phil Ochs was going to follow Bob Dylan's lead and evolve from a folksinger into a varied, world-class rock artist. And there was no reason to expect he should—perhaps one of the most unfair aspects of Ochs's legacy is the fact that he's been perpetually linked with Dylan. Ochs was a voice of political awareness, social justice, and fight-the-power spirit. It's a sad irony that a physical attack silenced the very voice that, at Ochs's peak, was unbowed by the oppression of censorship.

Roy

 ROCK AND ROLL HALL OF FAME
Inducted 1987

ACCIDENTS OF FATE

In 1963 Roy Orbison forgot his prescription glasses on an
airplane, and was forced to wear a pair of tinted glasses in order
to see. He had to leave immediately for a U.K. tour, where he was
warmly received and photographed with his dark shades. Soon the
glasses became a trademark, and Orbison always wore them in public.

"IN DREAMS I WALK WITH YOU"

With his pale complexion, goggle-like glasses, ethereal singing voice, and repertoire of songs running the gamut from adolescent angst to… well, *even more* adolescent angst, Roy Orbison seemed like a rock star fallen to earth from another planet altogether. Orbison's case for normality wasn't strengthened by a generation's reintroduction to his music via the squirmy sight of a ghastly Dean Stockwell lip-synching to "In Dreams" in the camp horror film *Blue Velvet*. And Orbison's life story—one of wrenching personal loss followed by a last-minute triumph and a sudden, untimely end—only enhanced the seeming oddity of his legacy.

Roy Orbison's up-and-down rock 'n' roll career had just reached a peak of unexpected resurgence when the singer suffered a heart attack in his mother's bathroom on December 6, 1988. Orbison's life had been marked by the tragic deaths of close family members, and it seemed a cruel irony that he passed away the same year the public seemed to remember his talent and bestow upon him status of a legend.

Orbison's first peak was in the early to mid-sixties, when his trademark dramatic ballads—marked by his unmistakable falsetto voice—topped the American and British charts. He contributed "Only the Lonely," "Running Scared," "Crying," "Dream Baby," and "Pretty Woman" to the rock 'n' roll canon. He sustained a tragedy in equal proportion to his successes in 1966; he was riding motorcycles with his wife, Claudette, and she suffered a fatal collision with a truck. Two years later, Orbison's Nashville home caught fire while he was on tour in Britain; the two eldest of his three sons, Roy Jr. and Tony, died in the blaze.

Despite a few high-profile gigs and limited success with greatest-hits packages, Orbison seemed relegated to the oldies circuit when "In Dreams" was used in the David Lynch film *Blue Velvet* in 1986 and rekindled interest. Orbison rerecorded his greatest hits with contemporary production values, then participated in all-star band the Traveling Wilburys with Bob Dylan, George Harrison, Tom Petty, and Jeff Lynne. The record was a hit, and Orbison recorded new material with Lynne—the LP *Mystery Girl*—that would reach #5 after Orbison's death.

Orbison had undergone heart surgery in 1979, although reports indicated that he continued smoking after his operation. A new generation of rock 'n' roll fans had become infatuated with his distinctive voice through his new solo hits and tunes with the Wilburys when he suddenly died. The Wilburys would dedicate their next LP to "Lefty," the persona he adopted with the band. His contributions were missed on the next recording, which lacked the spark of the first and met with decreased critical and commercial success.

For his part, Orbison didn't want to be remembered as a tragic figure. Nine days before his fatal heart attack, he told writer Nick Kent, "I don't want to be intellectual about it, but you've got to somehow let the sorrows of the past go and become just another part of your experience. Looking back, I truly feel that I have spent most of my life in a state of genuine contentment." Well said for a man whose spectral voice echoes still in countless dreams.

ESSENTIAL LISTENING
In Dreams: The Greatest Hits
Mystery Girl

DID YOU KNOW?
Roy Orbison is rightfully considered a legend today, but his fortunes sagged so deeply in the seventies that in 1976 he played the Van-a-Rama car show in Cincinnati before a crowd of less than a hundred.

rbison

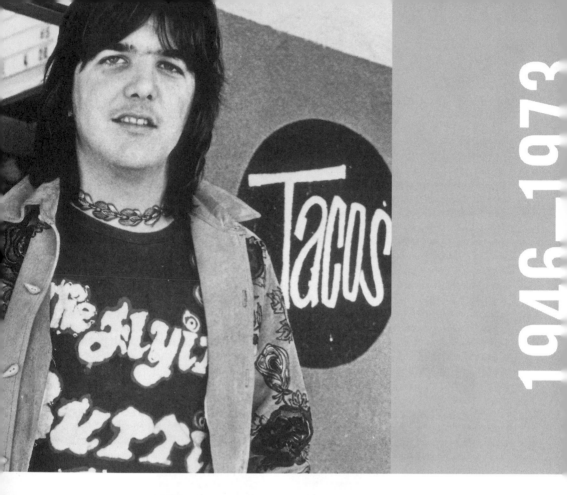

GRAM PARSONS

"We'll Sweep Out the Ashes in the Morning"

He was a country singer who carried himself with the defiant swagger of a rock star. He invented country rock, although he hated the term. He flitted from band to band, leaving behind some of the most vital music of the late sixties and early seventies. He influenced an entire genre of music decades after his death, although in life nothing he touched was ever much of a commercial success. He was Gram Parsons, pioneer and grand rock casualty.

Born Ingram Cecil Connor III (Gram was short for Ingram, not a variation of Graham as many supposed), Parsons grew up in luxury in Georgia as the son of an heiress and a WWII veteran named Coon Dog Connor. Parsons showed a strong interest in music as a boy, although at twelve his life was thrown into a tailspin by his father's suicide. His mother remarried the next year, and Robert Parsons adopted Ingram and legally changed the young man's name to Gram Parsons. The family left for Parsons's grandparents' home in Winter Haven, Florida.

Parsons played in bands through high school, then received another harsh blow when his mother died of alcohol poisoning the day he graduated from high school. Parsons continued with plans to attend Harvard, though after a single semester he left college and moved to the Bronx with his new group, the International Submarine Band. Parsons was playing country and R&B, beginning to fuse genres into what he would later refer to as "Cosmic American Music"—a term for which he campaigned in preference to "country rock," but that would find few other adherents.

In 1968 Parsons met Chris Hillman from the Byrds; the sixties megagroup had undergone sweeping personnel changes and was seeking a new direction. Parsons joined up for the LP *Sweetheart of the Rodeo*, a radical country departure from the Byrds's previous chiming guitars. The record contained the classic Parsons tune "Hickory Wind," but America wasn't avidly awaiting a country-rock fusion from the band who had provided "Turn! Turn! Turn!" two years before. Parsons was a member of the Byrds for only a few months; he apparently quit over an antiapartheid refusal to play a tour of South Africa.

The Byrds' Hillman saw where Parsons was going with his new music—into terrain that incorporated the traditional forms of country music while absorbing the swagger, edge, and contemporary relevance of the best rock 'n' roll. The pair formed the Flying Burrito Brothers and released *The Gilded Palace of Sin* in 1969. The record unveiled an adventuresome, tuneful new sound that both rock and country audiences managed to overlook almost completely. The record was a commercial bomb, and the next year Parsons left.

By this time Parsons was cutting quite a rock 'n' roll figure, with long hair, a piercing gaze, and surreal psychedelic suits such as the one sported on the cover of *Gilded Palace*. He attracted the attention and respect of rock 'n' rollers—most notably Keith Richards, with whom Parsons stayed in France while the Rolling Stones recorded *Exile on Main Street*. Parsons would soon record a version of the Stones' "Honky Tonk Women," a song he reportedly influenced. By this time Parsons was consuming enough liquor and hard drugs to hold his own with such legendary abusers as the Stones, which contributed to his aura of rock 'n' roll decadence.

In 1973 Parsons finally released a new record, *GP*, which featured singer Emmylou Harris (who sang aching duets with Parsons and would go on to become one of the greatest torch carriers for his memory) and members of Elvis's band. The record was consistently excellent, and consistently ignored. Parsons toured with his band the Fallen Angels and, in 1974, recorded the equally exemplary *Grievous Angel*. Immediately following its completion, Parsons overdosed on morphine and alcohol at a retreat near the Joshua Tree National Monument. Parsons's remains were being prepared for burial when friends recalled him expressing a preference for cremation at Joshua Tree. In a display of fraternal love, road manager Phil Kaufman got drunk, stole Parsons's body from the Los Angeles airport, returned Parsons to Joshua Tree, and set him afire.

With that, Gram Parsons was gone. It would be up to the Eagles to become country-rock zillion sellers—though Parsons arguably might never have embraced the pop sensibility that led to that group's dominance in the seventies. Parsons left behind a few vital recordings that remain truly original and enduring. His legacy also grew in the eighties and nineties, when several waves of new groups discovered his music and emulated his sound. In time the new genre came to be called "alt-country," though one imagines Parsons evincing as much distaste for it as he reserved for labeling his music "country rock." As he would have wished, we remember Parsons for his innovations in Cosmic American Music.

ROB PILATUS

"Blame It

What a terrible, terrible mess.

Milli Vanilli enjoyed several months of massive pop stardom in 1989, enjoying three #1s, massive exposure on MTV, and a high-profile tour that made Rob Pilatus and Fabrice Morvan household names. It was everything they'd ever dreamed of, except for one nagging detail—they lived in constant fear that the world would discover they hadn't sung a note on their records or in their concerts. They were frauds, and when they were exposed in 1990 they became the object of cruel mockery, lawsuits, and universal derision. Attempts at establishing any subsequent legitimacy met with total failure, and Pilatus descended into a hell of drug addiction, depression, and bizarre behavior that led him to an early grave.

The fiasco started in the mid-eighties, when German-born Pilatus met Morvan and decided to attempt a musical career as a duo. They released a 1986 album that went nowhere, then hooked up with Munich record producer Frankie Farian. Farian looked at the fit and photogenic duo, compared them with an unattractive but talented singing group he'd just recorded, and came up with an idea that must have seemed like a stroke of genius at the time. Using the best attributes of each act, Farian combined Pilatus and Morvan's good looks

on the Rain"

with a slick recording of "Girl You Know It's True" on which the duo had not appeared. It was perhaps a natural extension of using session substitutes to augment weak-voiced and unskilled pop stars, a practice as old as rock 'n' roll itself. But by not featuring Pilatus or Morvan on the resulting LP in any way, it was an act that was tantamount to fraud.

Pilatus and Morvan, desperate for a break and holding out hopes of actually singing on their next record, consented to becoming Milli Vanilli. What followed shocked them. They danced and lip-synched the song, filmed a video, and became an overnight success. The *Girl You Know It's True* LP was quickly recorded after its namesake single reached #2. Three chart toppers and a Grammy for Best New Artist followed. Pilatus and Morvan dove headfirst into their newfound stardom, waiting all the while for their ticket to be punched.

It didn't take long. Rumors swirled around Milli Vanilli almost from the beginning. At one concert appearance the backing CD they mimed to started to skip, forcing a humiliated Pilatus and Morvan to scramble offstage. By the end of 1989 they confirmed that they hadn't sung on their records or at live shows. Milli Vanilli's Grammy was rescinded, and the lawsuits started to fly. The public outcry was vociferous, and Milli Vanilli became the butt of vicious jokes

for years to come. Pilatus in particular was devastated by this reversal of fortune, and suffered bouts of mental instability when attempts at recording legitimate vocals met with resounding commercial failure.

Pilatus subsequently plunged still deeper into drugs and despair. He was arrested for assault, and he attempted suicide in 1991. He was unable to overcome his drug addiction even after repeated attempts at rehab. Interviews filmed in the nineties show Pilatus as agitated, restless, and tormented by his past. He returned to Germany for another try at making a record with his old producer, but was discovered dead by Farian and Ingrid Segeith on April 3, 1998, in his hotel room near Frankfurt. His death was attributed to heart failure precipitated by alcohol and prescription medication.

Milli Vanilli were certainly culpable for their willingness to take part in rock music's greatest fraud. But they were also young, naive, and hungry for a break in the music business. Morvan seems to have landed on his feet, but Pilatus was never able to rebound from the shame of his tenure in Milli Vanilli. His death put a lamentable end to his story of one year of success followed by a decade of pain and despondency.

Jeff Porcaro

"Out of Love"

The passing of Toto drummer Jeff Porcaro in 1992 left stunned music fans regarding the green space in front of their homes with a newfound wariness after an allergic reaction to lawn pesticides was cited as the cause of his death. A month later, however, a coroner's report concluded that Porcaro had suffered a rocker's more prosaic fate.

Toto formed in the late seventies in L.A., the result of six respected session musicians deciding it would be more rewarding to have their own names on the back of a record for a change. Taking the name of Dorothy's dog in *The Wizard of Oz*, the band's first single—"Hold the Line"—was an immediate hit, and its accompanying debut album, imaginatively titled *Toto*, hit the Top 10. Porcaro and his bandmates continued to play sessions between Toto albums, remaining in demand as exemplars of the late-seventies to early-eighties mainstream rock sound.

In 1982 Toto enjoyed its shining moment. After topping themselves in the distinctive-title stakes with *Toto IV*, they saw the album hit #4. The singles "Rosanna" and "Africa" went massive. Subsequent releases in the eighties failed to reproduce the Grammy-grabbing success of 1982, but gold records and Top 40 chart status remained theirs.

In 1992, Porcaro and Toto had recorded a new album and were preparing to hit the road when Jeff fell ill after applying a chemical pesticide to his lawn. He was taken to the hospital, where his condition worsened. He was pronounced dead on August 5 at 8:36 P.M. in Los Angeles. Manager Larry Fitzgerald stated that Porcaro's death had resulted from an allergic reaction to the pesticide, and rockers the world over considered whether they should simply let the crabgrass take over and live to fight another day.

The next day Bruce Springsteen dedicated a concert performance of "Human Touch" to Porcaro. At Porcaro's funeral, recordings of Steely Dan's "Home at Last," "Deacon Blues," and "Third World Man" were played, along with Jimi Hendrix's "The Wind Cries Mary." At year's end Toto played a benefit in L.A. to set up a trust fund for Porcaro's children; George Harrison, Donald Fagen, Eddie Van Halen, Don Henley, and Boz Scaggs were in attendance.

A month after Porcaro's death, L.A. County Coroner Bob Dambacher contradicted the earlier reports that pesticides had felled the Toto drummer. According to the coroner's report, Porcaro had died as a result of hardening of the arteries caused by cocaine abuse. The toxicology report located no pesticides in Porcaro's body, locating instead cocaine and a cocaine chemical by-product.

ESSENTIAL LISTENING
Past to Present (compilation)
Toto IV

Denied #1
In Toto's 1982–1983 moment of glory, the group charted five singles and took home six Grammys. "Africa" was a #1 hit, and while its companion single, "Rosanna," was equally ubiquitous on radio and MTV, its chart ascension stalled at #2. It was denied top-dog status, it turns out, by fellow timeless classics "Eye of the Tiger" by Survivor, and "Don't You Want Me" by Human League.

1954–1997

ELVIS PRESLEY

1935-1977

ESSENTIAL LISTENING
The Number One Hits
Sun Sessions
Elvis Recorded Live on Stage in Memphis

"All Shook Up"

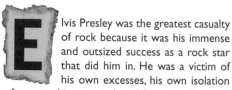

Elvis Presley was the greatest casualty of rock because it was his immense and outsized success as a rock star that did him in. He was a victim of his own excesses, his own isolation from anything normal, and his own distorted idea of stardom. The King's death was a tragedy because, by the time he died, he had strayed so far from the hard-rockin' musical god he once had been as to be unrecognizable as his former self. The original rock star stuffed himself with food and drugs until his body could take no more. He went from bloated self-parody to corpse without ever attaining a final moment of redemption.

Elvis grew up poor in Mississippi, and his family moved to Memphis in the late forties; there Elvis was exposed to the blues in addition to the standard fare of country and western. He was embarking on a career as a truck driver when, in the summer of 1953, he went into Sam Phillips's Sun Records studio and paid four dollars to make an acetate of himself singing two songs. Phillips soon realized what he had on his hands: a young white man who could reproduce the soul and grit of African-American blues and R&B. Elvis threw those styles into a pot with hillbilly country, added a dash of gospel, and invented what would soon be known as rock 'n' roll.

In 1956 Elvis got a deal with RCA records and became a star. In that one year he released two albums, performed on national television, starred in a movie (*Love Me Tender*), and put out a staggering string of hit records, including "Heartbreak Hotel," "Blue Suede Shoes," "Hound Dog," "Don't Be Cruel," and "I Want You, I Need You, I Love You." His crazy dancing and open sexuality—not to mention his beautiful face and slightly feminine pout—made him a figure of controversy and maniacal adulation. He was, at the time, the hottest-burning flame in all of popular music. He remained, at heart, a country boy from Mississippi, ill equipped to handle his unprecedented stardom.

The first of his many bad decisions was allowing Colonel Tom Parker to take over his management; in return for controlling Elvis's professional life from that day forward, Colonel Parker would receive a cool 25 percent of all Elvis's money—even after Elvis was dead. The next year Elvis bought Graceland, a twenty-three-room mansion in a Memphis suburb that would henceforth be the Buckingham Palace of the King's increasingly surreal world. The same year he released two #1 hits, "Jailhouse Rock"

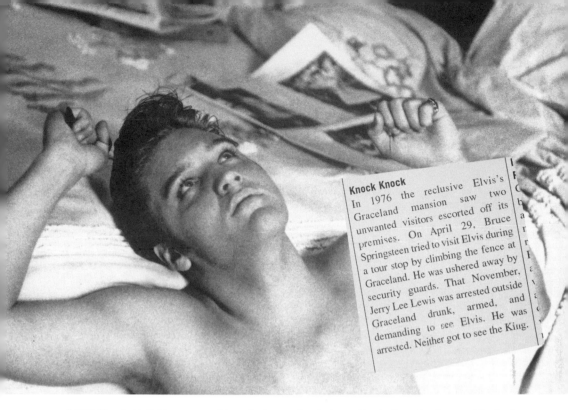

and "All Shook Up." He was working all the time, filming B movies, and recording constantly, in the process rapidly amassing a clutch of iconic, immortal singles that would constitute the greater part of his musical legacy.

In retrospect, it was in 1958 that things slowly started to go off the rails. He was drafted, and in March began basic training at Fort Hood, Texas. He recorded new tunes while on weekend furlough. In August of that year, his mother, Gladys, became ill with hepatitis. Elvis received a leave to return to Memphis to be with her, and she died nearly two weeks later. Elvis had always been very close to his mother, and her death devastated him. A couple of months later he was sent to Bremerhaven, West Germany, where he drove a jeep for his platoon sergeant. He would not return home until after his discharge in 1960. One by-product of Elvis's exile into military service was his acquaintance with Priscilla Beaulieu; she would move into Graceland in 1961, while still a teenager, and eventually marry Elvis.

Things had changed after Elvis got out of the army. He was still massively popular, but slowly the vitality seeped out of his music as Colonel Parker nudged him in the direction of highly profitable shlock. Elvis quit the stage and spent the sixties making bad movies. Some critics had been prepared to take Elvis seriously as an actor upon the release of his first couple of pre-army films—after all, who could deny his magnetism or his Brandoesque sneer? But after the army, Elvis plodded away on a treadmill of acting and producing music for as many as three films a year. Some of the soundtracks went gold, and there were hit singles along the way, but the danger and immediacy of Elvis at his best was replaced by airbrushed movie posters and tepid workaday sound tracks.

Something else happened along the way: the Beatles. The young Brits were five years or so younger than Elvis, and in 1964 they took over the King's mantle of biggest act in the world. Elvis spent his free time in Memphis, secluded in his mansion with his family and a selection of local cronies who came to be called the Memphis Mafia. Stardom can isolate even those who don't wish to be isolated, so what becomes of those who—like Elvis—seemed to crave a contraction of his world? The answer, of course: They slowly go out of their minds.

Elvis sensed what was happening to him, and he made a couple of valiant attempts at regaining his credibility. In 1968 he taped a TV special for NBC; Elvis and his stripped-down band played in the round, surrounded by a live audience. Elvis laughed, indulged in some self-deprecating humor, and gave a raw and mesmerizing performance. The show was aired that December and was a critical and ratings smash. Re-energized, Elvis recorded a handful of new songs and began a month-long residency at International Hotel in Las Vegas in July 1969. He was making money hand over fist in Vegas, and he enjoyed a few comeback hits—"Suspicious Minds," "In the Ghetto," "Don't Cry Daddy," and "Burning Love"—that stood alongside his fifties classics.

It was the seventies that were Elvis's final undoing. He returned to the road, and his records never stopped selling, but his life was falling apart. His marriage dissolved, and he sank deeper into drugs and social isolation. Though he didn't touch drink, he consumed an exponentially increasing volume of prescription medicines: tranquilizers, amphetamines, opiates. He could still sell out concerts, and his audience generally seemed oblivious to the fact that the star they idolized had totally lost it. He became obese, he sweated profusely, he forgot the words of his own songs and replaced them with bizarre, rambling ad-libs. The rolls of his fat were visible through the thick cloth and elaborate sequins of his increasingly baroque costumes.

Elvis developed health problems, and attempted drug treatment more than once to deal with his addictions. In 1975 he was hospitalized with hypertension and an impacted colon; part of his treatment included cortisone, which exacerbated Elvis's weight problem. In addition to his physical and mental difficulties, Elvis was having money worries—Colonel Parker's business deals had an uncanny way of benefiting Colonel Parker as much as Elvis, and the King's financial portfolio wasn't enhanced by his profligate spending and obliviousness to all things fiduciary. On August 1, 1977, *Elvis: What Happened?* was published; it was authored by two former members of the Memphis Mafia and contained an exposé of Elvis's increasing detachment from reality and elaborate eccentricities. The release of the book was fatefully timed, because Elvis wouldn't survive the month.

On August 16, at 2:20 in the afternoon, Elvis was discovered lying on the floor of an upstairs bathroom at Graceland. At the time of his death he had been seated on the toilet, perusing a book called *The Scientific Search for the Face of Jesus*. Two of his bodyguards tried to revive Elvis, but he was pronounced dead at 3:30 P.M. at Baptist Memorial Hospital in Memphis. His death at forty-two was attributed to heart failure. A toxicology test indicated that Elvis's bloodstream contained codeine, morphine, Quaaludes, and Valium, among other prescription controlled substances. Elvis's private doctor later faced charges of "indiscriminately prescribing 5,300 pills and vials" for the King over a seven-month period, but was acquitted.

The mythmaking around Elvis's memory began with his memorial service the day after his death, when twenty-five thousand fans filed past his coffin. His passing represented a sudden and stunning end for the generation that had raised him up as the greatest star of his day. Lower-rung tabloids would publish stories of Elvis sightings for the next twenty years, thus cementing his stature as one of American culture's most important and enduring figures. Legend, casualty, sometime apparition: Elvis Presley.

How Not to Manage a Rock Star, Parts 1 & 2

Colonel Tom Parker essentially barred Elvis from performing abroad, and except for his stint in the military Elvis stayed stateside. The reason? Apparently unbeknownst to Elvis, Colonel Parker was an illegal alien from Holland (his birth name was Andreas Cornelius van Kuijk) and feared dealing with immigration officials. Thus audiences around the world were deprived of an opportunity to see the King. Parker made another legendary gaffe in 1974, when he turned down an offer for Elvis to costar alongside Barbara Streisand in the hit remake of *A Star Is Born*. Parker said that Streisand didn't rate equal billing with Elvis, thus depriving him of a career-revitalizing opportunity.

The Pretenders
"I Found a Picture of You"

The voice, spirit, and driving force behind the Pretenders is and has always been Chrissie Hynde—a classic front woman and die-hard rock chick whose muse transcends musical genre and gender clichés to distill a blend of sixties rock, classic R&B, and the middle-finger-upraised rebellion of punk. Her music is that of a true student of rock, with an intimate knowledge of its history and conventions. But during a ten-month period in the early eighties, her band was visited by two deaths that ensured the Pretenders would never again be precisely the same unstoppable beast that had emerged at the dawn of that decade.

Hynde, born in Akron, Ohio, traveled to England to pursue a dream that failed to take root in the Midwest. She wrote reviews for the *New Musical Express*, and worked in Malcolm McLaren's shop called Sex a couple of years before that impresario latched onto the Sex Pistols and changed British music forever. Hynde played in bands and saw her peers—including the Damned and the Clash—seize fame and stardom in late-seventies punk. Finally, in 1978, she assembled the Pretenders, which included Pete Farndon on bass, James Honeyman-Scott on lead guitar, and Martin Chambers on drums.

James Honeyman-Scott
1957–1982

Pete Farndon
1953–1983

Her three bandmates were from Hereford—west of London, almost all the way to Wales. The group clicked quickly, with a sound based on Hynde's distinctive vocal texture, Honeyman-Scott's sixties-drenched guitar leads and chord structures, and Chambers's tight, workmanlike drumming. Added to the mix were Hynde's tough glamour and Farndon's screw-it rock-star posturing, and the Pretenders hit the U.K. charts at #34 in 1979 with a cover of the Kinks' "Stop Your Sobbing."

The next year the Pretenders became stars. "Brass in Pocket" topped the U.K. charts, and their debut album reached #1 in the U.K. and #9 in the U.S. The band toured America and played in Canada's Heatwave Festival before a crowd of fifty thousand. By 1981, *Pretenders II* hit the U.S. Top 10 and Hynde was fast becoming an icon. They charted brilliant singles such as "Kid," "Message of Love," and "Talk of the Town" that combined Hynde's biting lyrics and sensual vocals with Honeyman-Scott's chiming guitar sound. They quickly moved to the forefront of new wave, and were discovered by millions as a band accessible to both punk kids and older fans yearning for the melodicism of the sixties.

Success swatted the Pretenders swiftly and severely. Money and fame washed over a group that had been struggling just months before. The road-hardened Pretenders were no strangers to drugs and drink, and they now had the license of money and notoriety, combined with the pressures of chart success and hard touring, to fuel their bad behavior.

In May 1980, Hynde got into a fight with a Memphis bouncer and spent a night in jail. In October 1981, Martin Chambers put his hand through a window in Philadelphia and severed tendons and arteries—resulting in the cancellation of the final leg of a Pretenders tour. And, by most accounts, during this time James Honeyman-Scott and Pete Farndon were developing serious problems with hard drugs. The

members of the band weren't kids—by the time success found them, most had turned or were about to turn thirty. But the perils of the rock lifestyle were too much to resist.

By 1982 the Pretenders were no longer getting along with one another. It was the classic story: drugs, booze, egos, and too many adjustments for four personalities to handle while still meshing as a unit. On June 15, Pete Farndon was fired—the band said he was no longer compatible as a bandmate. The next day, June 16, James Honeyman-Scott died of a drug overdose. He was the youngest member of the Pretenders, still a few years shy of his thirtieth birthday. In a span of hours, the Pretenders had been reduced from four members to two. And the band was now deprived of a guitar technician who had played no small part in forging the group's distinctive sound.

The Pretenders would never be finished, though, as long as Hynde was still kicking. The group re-formed with ex-Rockpile guitarist Billy Bremner and recorded "Back on the Chain Gang," which reached #5 in 1983. One month later, exiled bass player Pete Farndon was found dead in his bathtub of apparent heart failure brought on by drugs.

The group's next album, *Learning to Crawl*, would hit the Top 10 and spark a successful tour and Top 40 singles. But the Pretenders were now a different animal—and as time passed, they became less of a band and more of a vehicle for Hynde's compositions and vocals. Varying degrees of success followed for the Pretenders. Only a fool would ever bet against Hynde's talent, her songs, or the trump card of her one-of-a-kind vox, but few would deny that things were never really the same. Drug abuse and excess had felled two of the founders of one of rock's all-time great bands, leaving its brilliant leader to spend the next two decades picking up the pieces without them.

Joey Ramone

1952–2001

"Too Tough to Die"

New Yorker Jeffrey Hyman was the unlikeliest of rock stars—he didn't have much of a voice, he was tall and gangly, and his features were perpetually obscured by a rat's nest of stringy black hair and dark sunglasses. But when he took the stage as Joey Ramone, front man of one of rock's greatest primitive innovative bands, he forever transformed the very idea of the rock 'n' roll star. By the time of his death from lymphoma in 2001, he was idolized as a grandfather of punk, following an unlikely quarter century in the public eye.

The Ramones emerged as though from some primordial stew in 1974, when they began a residency at famed Manhattan punk-rock petri dish CBGB's. Joey had recently stepped out from behind the drum kit to assume lead vocal duties, fronting a group that included Johnny, Dee Dee, and Tommy Ramone. Were they really brothers? Of course not, it was a put-on. But the Ramones looked as though they might have been the result of some genetic engineering experiment gone terribly awry; scruffy, loud, unapologetically moronic, they presented a united front of insolence in the face of the prevailing prog-rock pomposity. Their music was stripped down to three (sometimes two) chords of roaring noise, with songs that hardly lasted long enough to bark out a couple of choruses about suburban alienation and glue-sniffing angst before they abruptly terminated. Audiences were granted scarce recovery time before the next number began.

At the time, the question was how seriously the Ramones were to be taken—more to the point, how seriously did they take themselves? The answer might be found in the no-nonsense, raw-power fashion with which they introduced their songs onstage: with a clipped "1–2–3–4," followed by a sound that approximated an aged aircraft struggling to take wing. The Ramones had a sense of humor about themselves, but their limitless energy and mission to strip rock 'n' roll down to its essence were the result of a pure vision as much as of their acknowledged musical limitations.

The Ramones were a tonic to the introspective, symphonic pretensions of the time. They also opened a door through which such bands as the Sex Pistols, the Clash, and the Damned eagerly stepped through. Although the band's primary achievement was their audacious simplicity, the Ramones' secondary genius was their gift with song titles. Who could resist the considerable lure of tunes called "I Wanna Be Sedated," "Gimme Gimme Shock Treatment," "Cretin Hop," and "Teenage Lobotomy"?

Though few might have expected it, the Ramones were built to last. Throughout lineup changes and a general inability to transcend cult status, Joey Ramone continued to man the microphone well into the nineties. The Ramones were something like a strange sun around which other bands orbited; though they would tweak their essential sound with various experiments (including a 1980 collaboration with Phil Spector that the band would later repudiate), they would return time and again to their unrestrained energy of their basic approach. Finally the group called it a day in the mid-nineties, when the pop success of punk imitators became too much for pioneer Joey Ramone to bear. Joey enjoyed a few years as elder statesman before falling ill in 1998. He was diagnosed with lymphoma, a form of cancer, and succumbed in 2001 at the age of forty-nine. He's remembered as a true rock innovator who, with the Ramones, made an invigorating racket that sounds as true and vital now as when it was recorded.

 **ESSENTIAL LISTENING**
Ramones Mania (compilation)

1941–1967

ROCK AND ROLL HALL OF FAME
Inducted 1989

OTIS
Redding

"Sweet Soul Music"

Otis Redding was a dynamo singer and songwriter of unparalleled ability who established himself by the mid-sixties as one of a handful of premiere American R&B talents. After a blistering performance at a major rock festival, he was poised to conquer a wider audience when he died in a plane crash. He would never live to see the release of his biggest hit.

Born in Georgia, the son of a Baptist minister, Redding was of a perfect age to absorb the groundbreaking work of Sam Cooke, and while in his teens he played in Little Richard's backing group. After a handful of lesser releases and career misfires, he got a contract with industry giant Atlantic Records's Stax label in 1962. In his first sessions he recorded his tune "These Arms of Mine," which was a Top 20 R&B hit and established his solo career.

He was a prolific writer and a superb performer, blessed with a gritty emotive voice and the ability to stir an audience into a state of frenzy. By the mid-sixties he enjoyed an amazing string of hits that charted higher and higher on the pop charts while regularly cracking the R&B Top 10. He wrote or cowrote hits such as "Fa-Fa-Fa-Fa-Fa (Sad Song)," "Mr. Pitiful," "I've Been Loving You Too Long," and "Respect." The latter would later top the charts in a cover by Aretha Franklin. Redding also charted hits with Sam Cooke's "Shake" and the Rolling Stones's "Satisfaction."

In June of 1967, Redding made his bid for reaching the hippie audience when he played the Monterey Pop Festival. He closed the second evening, taking the stage after the Jefferson Airplane. A crowd more accustomed to the space-out stylings of the Grateful Dead and the Airplane were reportedly galvanized by Redding's R&B-rock fusion. It was an intriguing crossover; part of his set was released two years later on the LP *Otis Redding/Jimi Hendrix Experience*, on which each artist occupied an album side as a record of their Monterey performances.

Redding, like his idol Sam Cooke, had plans to expand his interests into his own record label, production, and management. But his life was cut short on December 10, 1967, when his chartered airplane crashed into Wisconsin's Lake Monoma; Redding perished along with every member of his backing band save one. A song he had cocomposed and recorded four days earlier—"(Sittin' on) The Dock of the Bay"—would be released after his death, topping the charts. The next year a greatest-hits compilation would outsell all his previous releases, as a mass audience discovered and reveled in the work of a great artist who had perished too soon.

ESSENTIAL LISTENING
Otis Blue/Otis Redding Sings Soul
Complete and Unbelievable . . . The Otis Redding Dictionary of Soul

A Job's a Job
In the early sixties, Otis Redding intermittently played local gigs in Macon with Johnny Jenkins & the Pinetoppers. He took the vocal spotlight for certain numbers in the group's live repertoire—and when he wasn't onstage he served as a chauffeur for the group.

Keith Relf

1943–1976

🏆 ROCK AND ROLL
HALL OF FAME
The Yardbirds inducted 1992

"Still I'm Sad"

 ESSENTIAL LISTENING
The Yardbirds: *Greatest Hits Vol. 1 (1964–1966)*
The Ultimate Collection

Keith Relf was a London-born singer who manned the microphone for the Yardbirds, the mid-sixties breakthrough blues-rock band that bred hall-of-fame guitarists and laid down the groundwork for the heavy rock of the seventies. The Yardbirds first formed in 1963 as a strict traditional blues band; they toured Europe and developed a strong following among blues-obsessed British youth.

In 1965 the Yardbirds enjoyed their first international success with "For Your Love." It was a fairly great single, combining elements of rock, blues, and psychedelia. Its pop success discouraged their guitarist, young Eric Clapton, who quit the group soon after. He was replaced by fledgling guitar deity Jeff Beck, and the hits "Heart Full of Soul," "Shapes of Things," and "Over Under Sideways Down" followed. The next year bass player Jimmy Page was promoted to co–lead guitarist alongside Beck. This lasted only a few months, ending with Beck's departure in the fall of 1966.

Relf was still on board, a white blues singer capable of bending his gruff pipes around pop and heavy rock, but after Beck's exit the Yardbirds listed badly. Subsequent releases failed to garner much attention, and the band sensed that their momentum might be stalled forever. The Yardbirds broke up in 1968. Clapton, Beck, and Page would all go on to big-time rock stardom in the seventies.

As for Relf, he formed the folk duo Together with fellow Yardbird Jim McCarty. Relf and McCarty's next move was to form the arty Renaissance, a group that tasted fame only after the two Yardbirds had long since departed. By this time Led Zeppelin's dinosaur stomp was being heard around the world, and Relf tried to follow suit with the heavy Armageddon (they had *better* be heavy with a name like that). Success remained elusive for Relf; then, on May 14, 1976, Relf became one of the oddest casualties of rock 'n' roll when he died at his home from electrocution while playing an electric guitar. This strange demise was deemed a freak accident.

RANDY RHOADS

"You Can't Kill Rock 'n' Roll"

1956–1982

I n the late seventies, Ozzy Osbourne had fallen upon a particularly dire predicament. He was no longer welcome in Black Sabbath, the band he had fronted in high-evil style for a decade. The public and press had pretty much written him off. He was sodden with booze and drugs, leaving the curtains drawn in his room and passing most days in a funk of inebriation and depression. Then two people came along to pull him out of his quagmire: Sharon Arden, his manager's daughter and Ozzy's future wife, and diminutive six-string hero Randy Rhoads. Ozzy's stunning comeback in 1980 owed plenty to Rhoads's pioneering metal wizardry, and it was a crushing blow when the guitarist was killed in a freak accident two years later.

Rhoads was born in Santa Monica into a musical family and started playing guitar while still a child. Upon the onset of adolescent hormones he took a strong interest in the heavy metal of the day, exemplified by Led Zeppelin, Black Sabbath, and the theatrical excesses of Alice Cooper. Rhoads continued to study the guitar and enrich his knowledge of music even as he joined up with L.A.'s Quiet Riot in the late seventies. He developed a virtuosic touch, and became one of the first guitarists on the scene to incorporate classical scales and techniques into his playing.

Quiet Riot seemed stalled out after failing to secure an American record deal (it would be a couple of years yet before the next incarnation of the group hit the charts with lunk-headed Slade covers), and when Rhoads heard Ozzy was auditioning guitarists for a new LP and band he duly attended tryouts and wrested away the job from a platoon of wanna-bes. In 1980 Ozzy released *Blizzard of Ozz*. By this time few expected quality work from Osbourne, but he confounded expectations by coming up with one of the greatest metal albums of all time. Rhoads's signature was all over the album, particularly on the single "Crazy Train," which featured a hall-of-fame riff and a guitar solo that earned Rhoads a permanent place in the guitar-god pantheon.

Blizzard of Ozz was a hit, and Rhoads hit the road with Ozzy. The next year saw the release of *Diary of a Madman*, which nearly equaled its predecessor. Although Rhoads said he hadn't done his best work on the record due to a tight deadline, his playing on it was nothing short of phenomenal. Ozzy was back in a big way, and Randy Rhoads was a vital cog in the new machine. His status as hero for those who favored headphones, locked bedroom doors, and pages of scales was cemented in 1981 by Rhoads's election as Best New Guitarist by *Guitar Player* magazine.

The possibilities seemed endless for Rhoads; then, on March 19, 1982, he was killed when the band's tour plane descended on the tour bus as a joke. The plane's wing clipped the bus, and the craft spiraled out of control and crashed into a house. Rhoads, who was in the aircraft, died in the accident, along with pilot Andrew Aycock and tour hairdresser Rachel Youngblood. In 1987 Ozzy released *Tribute,* a collection of live recordings featuring Rhoads; it was a Top 10 success. In the years since, the excesses of metal guitarists with classical pretensions have been justly jeered at, but in his day Randy Rhoads was an inventive pioneer who left a legacy of outsized proportions, considering the scarcity of his recorded work.

 ESSENTIAL LISTENING
With Ozzy Osbourne: *Blizzard of Ozz*
Diary of a Madman

Mark Sandman

Morphine front man Mark Sandman led a group that forged a rock 'n' roll sound that without exaggeration could be described as unique—in lieu of guitars, their sound was held together by a throbbing two-string bass and raucous saxophone. The result was a rush of blues, jazz, and rock that Sandman topped off with intelligent, acerbic lyrics.

Formed in Boston in 1990, Morphine came to semiprominence in 1993 with the release *Cure for Pain*, which garnered the band mainstream attention and sold well for an independent release. After tours and a follow-up LP, Morphine had solidified a loyal cult following. In 1996 the group signed up with the major label Dreamworks, but the critically lauded *Like Swimming* failed to reach a mass audience. On July 3, 1999, tragedy struck when Sandman collapsed onstage in Rome during a performance. He was dead of a heart attack at forty-seven. Sandman's devoted audience continue to enjoy posthumous releases and make Morphine a popular subject of conversation on the Internet.

Bon Scott

had the unique ability to convey a leer and a wink in his voice from the dark grooves of a hard-rock LP. As the original singer for AC/DC, he contributed to the formulation of a new sound: raw, stripped-down, riff-driven, with vocals steeped in shots of hard liquor and, one might have thought, measures of industrial-strength drain cleaner. His untimely death left AC/DC confused and adrift. By the end of the year the band would regroup for its greatest triumph.

Like the Young brothers Malcolm and Angus—the heart and soul of AC/DC—Bon Scott (b. Ronald Belford) was an immigrant to Australia from Scotland. Bon had played in Australian groups since the mid-sixties, joining the Young brothers in 1973. Bon was more than a decade older than his new bandmates, and his position as deranged honorary older brother was cemented by his previous criminal convictions and the cachet of having been declared "socially maladjusted" by the Australian Army.

Bon Scott and AC/DC were not an overnight sensation; they toiled to establish an audience in Australia before signing with Atlantic Records in 1976 and moving to the U.K. They were making records that would become well known in the U.S. only in retrospect: "TNT," "Dirty Deeds Done Dirt Cheap," and the jaw-dropping adolescent prurience—and twisted greatness—of "Big Balls" and "The Jack." In 1979, the band established themselves at the forefront of their hard-rock class. AC/DC's LP *Highway to Hell*, with its scathing title track, hit #17 in the U.S. and was the band's first million seller. They had already played big venues in

1946–1981

Heartbreak of a Rocker
"When you're younger you don't think that something like death is going to touch you. I'd never really had a tragedy that close, and especially someone like Bon . . . that was just one of those things where one day somebody is there and it's so hard to believe the next day they're not there."

—Angus Young

"Hell's Bells"

Australia and the U.K., and now they moved from the club circuit in America to a tour supporting Cheap Trick and Ted Nugent—two of the highest-profile acts of the day.

AC/DC's music was hard, raunchy, and debauched. The men who created it fit the same profile. Bon Scott's hard-bitten, virile image was no publicist's invention, and he was on a first-name basis with rough living and two-fisted drinking. He was a tough guy and a survivor, and those who knew him were stunned when he suddenly died.

On February 19, 1980, AC/DC were recording a new album in London; the group was laying down backing tracks and was almost ready for Scott to join them and begin composing lyrics. Scott went out that night with friend Alistair Kennear, watched a couple of live bands, and—nothing unusual—drank a large amount of alcohol. When they reached Kennear's house at the end of the evening, Kennear left Bon Scott in the car to sleep off the effects of the night's booze consumption. When he came out the next morning, Scott was inert. He was pronounced dead at nearby King's College Hospital. The coroner would state that Bon Scott had drunk himself to death; he had apparently choked to death on his own vomit while unconscious.

AC/DC was left without a voice, a founding member, and a friend who had become a brother. It seemed likely that Scott's death would end the group. Somewhat improbably, the Young brothers and their bandmates soon hired a new singer—Brian Johnson, with his ultramanly howling powerhouse of a voice—and finished the LP that would be called *Back in Black* in honor of Bon Scott. By 1997 *Back in Black* had sold sixteen million copies. AC/DC was bigger than ever, and the old LPs with Scott began to chart as well.

Bon Scott was a talented and tough-as-nails hard-rock singer, and, although the band has now been together with Brian Johnson longer than with its original vocalist, his memory will always shadow AC/DC. In fact, they released a five-CD box set called *Bonfire* in 1997 as a tribute.

TUPAC SHAKUR

1971–1996

ESSENTIAL LISTENING
Greatest Hits
2Pacalypse Now

"THUG LIFE"

upac Shakur was one of the most conflicted and contradictory figures in nineties pop music; multitalented and oozing charisma, he combined parallel careers as a film star and hip-hop artist while seeming to embody the struggles of African Americans of his generation. Trouble swirled around him like a cloud that wouldn't lift—most of it his own doing—and he was gunned down in Las Vegas at the age of twenty-five. He left a handful of lasting tracks and the lingering question of whether his murder was linked to a deadly series of events springing from a rap-world rivalry.

Shakur was born in New York; his mother was Afeni Shakur, a Black Panther activist. The conflicts in his soul started early—while he grew up knowing African-American revolutionaries, steeped in philosophies of radical liberation, his everyday reality comprised welfare dependence and a crack-smoking mother. Shakur was very bright and artistic from an early age, and after he and his mother relocated from New York, he studied acting and dance at Baltimore's School for the Arts. His early ambitions were defeated, though, when his mother moved again, this time to Marin City, California. There he left home at sixteen and began running with drug dealers and gangs. Shakur was hardened by experience, and would retain his loyalty to the Darwinian violence and brutality of gang-banging until the end of his life—it was termed "thug life," which Shakur would have tattooed across his sculpted torso in case anyone failed to apprehend where he was coming from.

In the early nineties Shakur worked as a dancer for Digital Underground, a Bay Area hip-hop group, and soon landed a record deal that resulted in his debut, *2Pacalypse Now*, which was an immediate hit. The next year he starred in the Hollywood film *Juice* as a violent gangsta named Bishop. The role would be instrumental in cementing Shakur's worldview; he would later admit that "Bishop just never left me." With a hit record and film under his belt, Shakur was in an enviable position. But his very success depicting the conditions of American ghetto life affirmed and hardened the aspect of his personality that embraced criminality and violence; while he was a sensitive young man with a poetic soul, he locked into the anger and rage that erupt from poverty and repression. He was an iconic figure to young African Americans, but instead of choosing to channel that adoration into a tenable vision of transcendence and concrete revolution—the goal of his spiritual forefathers in the Black Panthers—Shakur opted to, in essence, let the dark side take over.

Maybe he simply felt he had to live up to his persona as a doomed bad boy. Legitimacy in some hip-hop quarters meant holding tight to a criminal past and present, and Shakur embarked on that route with a vengeance. He was charged yet not convicted of involvement in shootings in 1992 and 1993; soon after came sexual assault charges and a jail stay after Shakur assaulted movie director Allen Hughes. In 1994 Shakur was shot in the lobby of a New York recording studio—it soon surfaced that two of Shakur's hip-hop enemies, Sean "Puffy" Combs and Notorious B.I.G., were also in the building at the time. Talk of a rivalry between East Coast and West Coast rap factions turned increasingly contentious and abusive.

Shakur released subsequent hit albums with titles that reflected his incendiary, dangerous image: *Strictly for My N.I.G.G.A.Z.* and *Me Against the World*. Sometimes lost amid Shakur's image and thuggish rhetoric was the evolution of a distinctive talent. Shakur's records sold on the merits of his deft, witty compositions combined with his deep voice and melodic rapping style. They also sold on the back of his defiant stance against order and authority, which was amplified in 1996, when—following a yearlong stay at New York's Riker's Island after a sexual-assault conviction—Shakur entered the camp of Death Row Records and Suge Knight. Knight's roster of artists wore their gang connections on their sleeves, and soon a prevailing theme of his work was viciously taunting East Coast rappers.

By many accounts, Death Row Records was run like a gang-style enterprise, with intimidation and beatings replacing more subtle forms of negotiation. Shakur entered into a partnership with the hardest, meanest, most dangerous faction of the recording industry. He embodied the glorification of gangs, drug dealers, and ghetto nihilism. If the flame of controversy ever seemed in danger of going out, Shakur would pour gasoline upon it; perhaps his most infamous provocation came in a lyric in which Shakur boasted of having sex with Notorious B.I.G.'s wife. Shakur goaded and gloated, generally behaving as though he were unreachable and invincible.

Any illusions of that sort came to a lamentable termination on September 7, 1996. While riding in Suge Knight's car in Las Vegas, Shakur was struck by a hail of bullets, two of which punctured his lungs. Shakur battled his injuries for six days in the hospital until he was pronounced dead. Six months later Notorious B.I.G. was slain in Los Angeles. Many have linked the two shootings, Shakur's as reprisal for slights in the East Coast–West Coast war of words, Notorious B.I.G.'s as revenge, but neither case has been solved.

The tragedy of Tupac Shakur's death impacts on several levels. He was murdered while still a young man, intoxicated by his own fame and the lure of being the baddest of the bad. It's hard to imagine he wouldn't have eventually backed down from his thug-life stance and offered a more thoughtful and illuminating perspective. He was one of hip-hop's great talents, and his rage masked a sensitive, perceptive nature that might have crystallized into a distinctively African-American vision that could have, in some fashion, offered solutions to or solace from the tragedy of the American ghetto. Instead he fell for the lure of anger and the cold gratification of thug life. And it did him in.

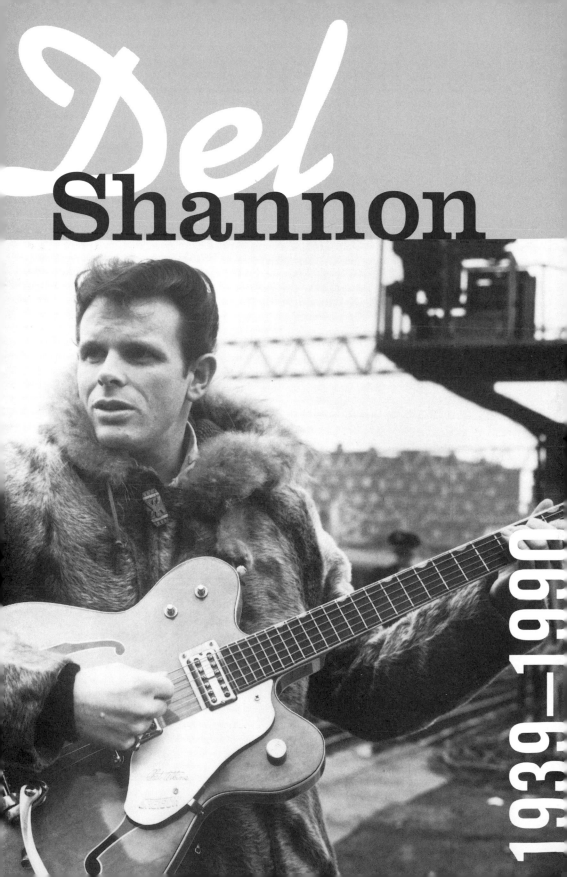

Del
Shannon

1939–1990

"So Long, Baby"

T hough he endured a series of career ups and downs, Del Shannon was one of the few survivors of rock's first generation who outlasted the arrival of the Beatles and continued to make new music into the eighties. Dogged by depression, his 1990 suicide sparked a controversy over the effects of antidepressant drugs.

Michigan's Charles Westover gained early performing experience playing armed-forces radio shows in West Germany. After he returned to civilian life he got a record deal and made two trips to New York to record. On the second the rechristened Del Shannon struck pay dirt with the eccentric single "Runaway." The song was a strange beast, with a Musitron solo predating synthesizers by a couple of decades, and a sped-up falsetto vocal by Shannon. It topped the U.S. and U.K. charts and made Shannon an international star. Follow-up "Hats Off to Larry" reached #5. Subsequent efforts—largely composed by Shannon—routinely reached the Top 40. Shannon was one of the few credible rockers to emerge in the period between Buddy Holly's death and the emergence of the Beatles.

The seventies saw Shannon step away from the microphone to pursue work as a record producer. Sporadic recordings followed, and by the late seventies reports surfaced that Shannon was battling alcoholism. In 1979 Shannon played a memorial show at the Surf Ballroom in Clear Lake, Iowa, to commemorate the twentieth anniversary of the deaths of Buddy Holly, Ritchie Valens, and the Big Bopper. Shannon performed occasionally on nostalgia tours, and collaborated with Tom Petty on the 1981 LP *Drop Down and Get Me*. The album failed to crack the Top 100, but the single "Sea of Love" reached the Top 40.

In the eighties Del Shannon may have been able to view his best work only in the rearview mirror, but he was reportedly financially secure and could still find audiences eager to hear his renditions of the old hits. Apparently these consolations were insufficient. In 1990, five days after playing another Holly tribute at Clear Lake, Del Shannon died at home from a self-inflicted gunshot wound to the head. Shannon had been battling internal demons and depression, and doctors had prescribed Prozac as treatment. A year after Shannon's suicide, his widow initiated court proceedings against the drug's makers; she claimed that Prozac had contributed to Shannon's suicidal frame of mind. Whatever the cause, Shannon had succumbed to demons within.

ROCK AND ROLL HALL OF FAME
Inducted 1999

ESSENTIAL LISTENING
Greatest Hits
Runaway (Golden Stars)

ESSENTIAL LISTENING
With Hillel Slovak: *Freaky Styley*
Post-Slovak: *Mother's Milk*
BloodSugarSexMagik

Hillel
slovak

The Red Hot Chili Peppers' boy's-town funk was one of the signature good-time sounds of the eighties, but a darker undertow tugged at the group in the form of heroin addiction. Though singer Anthony Kiedis and latter-day guitarist John Frusciante struggled with heroin habits, they were able to eventually clean up. Founding guitarist Hillel Slovak was not as fortunate.

In light of their breakthrough hits in the early nineties, it's easy to forget that the Chili Peppers were once a mediocre-selling cult band. They pioneered an unholy blend of funk, metal, and punk in the mid-eighties, but their 1987 release *The Uplift Mofo Party Plan* stalled at #148 on the charts. They were onto something, though, and developed a strong following from their incendiary live shows and lascivious image. No small factor in their emergence was guitarist Hillel Slovak, whose funky thrash guitar, along with the bass stylings of the entomologically nicknamed Flea (born Michael Balzary), defined the Chili Peppers' early sound.

Heroin had entered the picture by the mid-eighties, and it would almost destroy the band.

Behind the band's party-hard image were two band members in thrall to drug addiction. Hillel Slovak was found dead of an overdose in Los Angeles in 1988. Singer Kiedis was also addicted, a state of affairs that compelled drummer Jack Irons to exit the band. The Chili Peppers stalled out for a time, but eventually re-formed and released 1992's *BloodSugarSexMagik*, a #3 LP featuring the ballad "Under the Bridge," a Kiedis composition that earned the greatest commercial success of the group's career.

The hard times were by no means over, though. Soon Frusciante quit the group and lapsed into a deep heroin addiction of his own. The Chili Peppers soldiered on with mixed results, and in an improbable twist welcomed a cleaned-up Frusciante back to the fold in 1998 and released the hit LP *Californication* the next year. The Red Hot Chili Peppers have become a sort of musical institution, capable of greatness, and have proven to be made of sufficiently hardy stuff to endure the hardships of loss and addiction. The loss of friend and colleague Hillel Slovak remains a tragic note in their history.

Bob Stinson
"Here Comes a Regular"

The early eighties saw the Replacements emerge from the frozen urban landscape of Minneapolis—a group whose sound and ethos evoked postadolescent longing and the unique sensation of a bell-ringing hangover on a snowy morning. Their lead guitarist, Bob Stinson, steered their early charge with a playing style that combined heavy metal, punk, and glam rock in a blender from hell.

As the decade wore on, the early blitzed blitz of the Replacements' first recordings—including the pungent *The Replacements Stink*—gave way to a more polished approach spearheaded by the accomplished writing of Paul Westerberg. Mind you, this was still a group known for vomiting in the recording studio and lying onstage in a plastic wading pool full of dingy brown water. But Bob Stinson's own brand of excess was too much for the rest of the group, and he was expelled in 1986.

The Replacements went on to their own twisted brand of immortality, achieving fame and then imploding partly as a result of their discomfort with graduating to major-label entanglements. Bob Stinson reportedly did not thrive in his post-Replacements tenure; booze and drugs remained in the picture, new bands failed to leave the launching pad, and the guitarist's health began to erode badly. Bob Stinson died in Minneapolis in 1995, his body failing after more than a decade of hard abuse. A collection was taken up in hopes of placing a bench next to one of Stinson's favorite spots by a Minneapolis lake, a reminder of happier and more idyllic times.

 **ESSENTIAL LISTENING**
Let It Be
Hootenanny

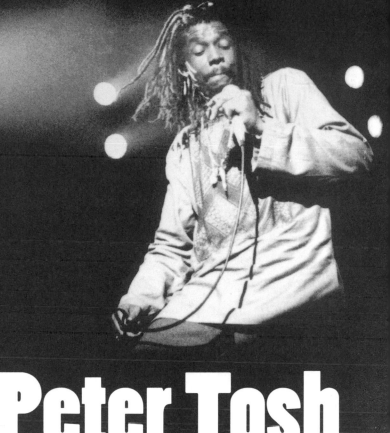

Peter Tosh

"Get Up, Stand Up"

Peter Tosh was a reggae bomb thrower, a voice for the dispossessed people of the Third World, and a tireless campaigner for his beloved *ganja*. Described as Malcolm X to Bob Marley's Martin Luther King, Jr., Tosh stepped out from the shadow of the Wailers for a turbulent solo career that mixed music with politics and led to savage beatings at the hands of Jamaican police. His brutal murder in 1987 came as a result of his generosity to the sort of outlaw he sometimes praised in song.

Born Winston Hubert MacIntosh, Peter Tosh came of age in Kingston's notorious Trenchtown, one of the most dangerous slums in the world. In the mid-sixties he formed the Wailers with friends Bob Marley and Bunny Livingston; the name of their band was meant to evoke the sense of mourning they and their fellow Trenchtown residents suffered in the

deprivation of their daily lives. Reggae music was one of the few consolations for black Jamaicans, and Tosh released solo singles as well as tracks
with the Wailers in the burgeoning Kingston music scene.

In 1966 Ethiopian monarch Haile Selassie visited Jamaica, and Tosh and
Marley became adherents of the Rastafarian religion, which taught that
Selassie was the messiah, that Africans were the chosen people of God,
and that biblical scripture had been manipulated to obscure the fact that
God was black. Another component of Rastafarianism was the hearty
consumption of *ganja*—strong marijuana—a practice that Tosh and
Marley enthusiastically embraced.

The Wailers' Jamaican success turned global in the early seventies,
when Island Records head Chris Blackwell signed them to his label and
began to aggressively promote reggae to American and European audiences. The Wailers' music was sensual and political, and their renown
grew quickly. Tosh sang colead with Marley on the early hit "Get Up, Stand
Up," but felt frustrated that his own material was being neglected in favor
of Marley's work. By 1974 the band was being billed as Bob Marley and
the Wailers, and Tosh was gone.

Tosh infused his subsequent music and life with a political sensibility
that bordered on revolutionary rage. He openly provoked authorities
onstage, and once reportedly drove a truck through a department store
window during a riot in Jamaica. The island was a land of inequity and
inequality, and Tosh was in the camp that advocated justice through any
means necessary. For his troubles Tosh was nabbed more than once on the
street by Jamaican police on marijuana charges and beaten nearly to death.

Reggae music in the second half of the seventies enjoyed a commercial
golden moment—largely on the strength of Bob Marley's universally
accessible songwriting and vast charisma—and Tosh enjoyed success as
well, albeit on a smaller scale. His sales were partly limited by his unflinching
convictions—the cover of his first solo LP, *Legalize It*, featured him in a
lush marijuana field, and his work began to pale in comparison to Marley's.
Tosh grew embittered in the face of his former bandmate's globe-trotting
success, and reacted by throwing himself deeper into his role as
spokesman for the planet's billions of oppressed people. His next LP, *Equal
Rights*, went gold.

Following a 1978 performance at the One Love Peace Festival in
Kingston, at which Tosh smoked a gargantuan spliff onstage and hectored
the prime minister for not legalizing *ganja*, Mick Jagger took note of the
crowd's enthusiastic reaction and signed Tosh to Rolling Stones records.
Bush Doctor followed; it featured a duet between Peter and Jagger on the
Temptations' "(You Got to Walk and) Don't Look Back." His association
with the Stones led to greater public visibility, but Tosh found himself in a
situation that typified his career: he was making records and touring, but
found himself with little money to show for his labors. His relationship
with the Stones soured after Tosh trashed a home owned by Keith
Richards in Jamaica as retaliation for perceived disrespect and broken

promises. Soon after Tosh received one of his brutal beatings from the police—this time, reportedly, as payback for his audacious challenge to authority at the One Love festival.

In 1981 Bob Marley died, leaving the reggae world without its breakthrough star. Tosh reacted badly, making disrespectful comments when he could have set a tone of reconciliation with his old partner. A period of personal decline followed, in which he smoked *ganja* heavily and began to blame Satan and evil spirits for the difficulties and frustrations of his life. In 1983 he withdrew from public life with his common-law wife Marlene, who some claimed isolated Tosh from old friends and stoked the fires of his considerable paranoia. After four years of relative seclusion, Tosh returned with *No Nuclear War*, another overtly political album.

A few months later, the violence that characterizes life in Jamaica intruded upon Tosh's life just as he was contemplating a return to the world stage. Tosh had always used his resources to help the poor, and one of his beneficiaries was a released convict named Dennis "Leppo" Lobban. On September 11, Tosh was having a get-together in his house with friends when Lobban and two armed accomplices arrived. What had been a happy event was soon tainted with menace and spilled blood.

The robbers began to beat Tosh, claiming to the alarm of the terrified guests that they were going to behead him. Tosh reportedly begged for his life, telling his assailants he had no money in the house but could get some if he was spared. Said Michael Robinson, present at the scene, "The last sentence that he said, his voice was all breaking up and showing nervousness. And he was stuttering, 'I can make some arrangements some other time.'"

The deadly situation spiraled out of control, and the gunmen opened fire on the roomful of people. Peter was murdered, along with two others. Four more were injured in the chaos. Lobban received a quick conviction and life sentence. The other two gunmen weren't found. While the apparent motivation for the attack was robbery, some speculated that Peter had been executed as a final reprisal for his continued attacks on authority. Whatever the case, Tosh lived a short and turbulent life, his oft-strident voice always keen to trumpet the causes of compassion and equality.

ESSENTIAL LISTENING
The Best of Peter Tosh
Equal Rights

"Soul to Soul"

Stevie Ray VAUGHAN

1954–1990

ESSENTIAL LISTENING
Greatest Hits
Texas Flood

Stevie Ray Vaughan's staggering prowess with the electric guitar brought him fame and fortune, along with a near-debilitating substance-abuse problem that dogged much of his peak years. He had conquered his addictions and attacked his music with a renewed focus when he died in a helicopter crash following an incendiary live performance.

Vaughan was a guitar prodigy in his teens, playing in bands with his older brother Jimmie and developing a ferocious psychedelic-blues style that encompassed influences from Jimi Hendrix to Albert King. Before long it was clear to anyone who listened that young Stevie Ray was the best player on nearly any stage he stepped onto, and after years of apprenticeship in Austin, Texas, he formed Double Trouble— the tight three-piece band that Vaughan would use as a vehicle to stardom.

The casual music fan first learned about Vaughan from his snaky guitar licks on David Bowie's 1983 megasmash *Let's Dance*; the same year Vaughan and Double Trouble released *Texas Flood*, a million-selling debut. Their next record, *Couldn't Stand the Weather*, went platinum. Vaughan's profile grew, as did his reputation as the newest master of the blues guitar. Vaughan's appeal crossed boundaries and quickly outgrew the small hard-core blues audience. His appeal was entirely a result of his inspired guitar playing—his style was emotive, technically impeccable, full of fire and life. When he played, all talk stopped.

But by the mid-eighties things had started to go wrong. Vaughan and Double Trouble were a hard-bitten road band, and their constant touring schedule was exhausting. Vaughan developed addictions, and his predilection for dissolving powder cocaine in a glass of whiskey as a morning pick-me-up nearly destroyed his stomach. What had started as a way of getting up for shows, then coming down afterward, turned into a near-fatal medical condition. He fell off a stage in London, and vomited blood on the street during a European tour. Success had come fast and hard for Vaughan, and suddenly it looked as though it might destroy him.

Vaughan proved to be made of resilient stuff; he checked into an Atlanta hospital in 1986 and completed a month of rehabilitation. He emerged revitalized, according to those who knew him, and burning with a desire to reconnect to the spiritual storm of his guitar playing. He began to relate his story during interludes in his stage performances, exhorting his audience to stay clean and face their own substance-abuse problems. Somehow he pulled it off; what might have sounded like rock-star preaching instead came across as a heartfelt plea for his fans to join him in sobriety and health.

Vaughan and Double Trouble received a Grammy for their 1989 LP, *In Step*, and Vaughan completed an album with his brother Jimmie (who enjoyed success of his own with the Fabulous Thunderbirds) in July of 1990 that would be called *Family Style*. On August 27 that year, Vaughan played a show at the Alpine Valley Music Theater in East Troy, Wisconsin. The concert ended with Vaughan jamming with Jimmie, Eric Clapton, Robert Cray, and Buddy Guy. Afterward Vaughan got into a helicopter bound for Chicago. It encountered thick fog and crashed into a man-made ski hill. Vaughan died along with Clapton's agent, the pilot, and Clapton's bodyguard.

With a quickness akin to Vaughan's high-speed fretboard runs, Stevie Ray was gone. He left behind a handful of albums, along with memories that burned in the recollections of the millions who saw him play. The end might have come too soon for Stevie Ray Vaughan, but he was at least clean and sober on the August day he lost his life. Vaughan faced down his demons and lived to see the other side, a triumph that will always color his legacy with warmer tones than those who failed.

1957–1979

Sid
Vicious

"Pretty Vacant"

Sid Vicious may or may not have been a danger to others, but he was certainly a danger to himself. He was accused of murdering his girlfriend but died of a drug overdose before he could stand trial. By most accounts, Vicious started out as a reasonably harmless soul who lacked the will and acuity to halt a rapid slide into a quagmire of hangers-on and drug addiction after he was invited to join the Sex Pistols. Punk rock was an enthusiastically upraised middle finger in the face of the complacent rock establishment, a rousing call for a stripped-down, adrenaline-drenched, egalitarian noise. It was also a breeding ground for aggressive stupidity, vandalism masquerading as rebellion, and dunderheaded negativity posing as iconoclasm. Sid Vicious was a staunch standard-bearer for the latter contingent.

The Sex Pistols were the first and greatest of the U.K. punk bands, formed in 1975, when John Lydon's personal grooming habits led to his rebirth as Johnny Rotten. Shop owner Malcolm McLaren assumed management of the fledgling group and prodded its members toward increasingly greater heights of outrage and repulsion. Their first single was released in December 1976. "Anarchy in the U.K." grazed the U.K. Top 40; in retrospect it was a ground-breaking moment in the history of rock 'n' roll. The music was stripped down and primal, driven by Steve Jones's rudimentary guitar and Rotten's snarling, jeering vocals. Rotten's proclamation "I am an Antichrist" jarred England with its antisocial bitterness.

By the next year the Sex Pistols were, depending on where one's loyalties were placed, either a national sensation or a horrible disgrace. They were crude, vulgar, and blatantly working-class, and could be goaded into all sorts of mischief. The British press reported on their daily outrages with predictable zeal. In March, the Sex Pistols responded by chewing off their own head—they sacked bass player Glen Matlock, their only real musician and their best songwriter. Despite his resounding inability to play a musical instrument, Rotten's chum Sid Vicious—named after a pet hamster—was invited to join the most notorious band in Britain.

Vicious—born John Simon Ritchie in London—would never have been enlisted in a band on the strength of his musical prowess. But Vicious had the right name and look for a group that feasted on media attention. While the Sex Pistols themselves came more or less as they were packaged—pissed-off young Brits facing a bleak future in a moment of national decline—their manager was scouting for choice seats on the gravy train. McLaren knew any publicity was good publicity, and by the time Vicious joined the fold the Sex Pistols were indulging in such orchestrated pranks as signing a new record deal in front of Buckingham Palace for obliging cameras. The Sex Pistols were turning into antistars, and Vicious was their man—staggering, his clothes ripped and hair spiked, his expression fixed with impudent, willful stupidity, Sid embodied the mindless destructiveness of punk with singular relish.

In May the Sex Pistols released "God Save the Queen" to coincide with the Queen's Silver Jubilee. The lyric, with Lydon sneering that the Queen "ain't no human being," earned the tune an instant ban from British radio. When it went to #2 on the charts, it was represented by an empty space in U.K. papers. The Sex Pistols had become genuine rock 'n' roll revolutionaries, garnering controversy in equal measure to the exhilarating brilliance of their music. "God Save the Queen," for all its calculated outlaw appeal, remains one of the greatest songs in rock 'n' roll history.

While it has been debated since whether the Sex Pistols' achievements were the conscious effort of a group of true social radicals or the accidental genius of four thugs and their evil

Svengali, no one has ever maintained that Sid Vicious accomplished much of anything in the band other than mayhem and posturing. He quickly plunged into hard drug abuse, and was noted for acts of violence and vandalism. Meanwhile, the Sex Pistols' story started to turn dark when various band members were attacked on London streets by club-and-razor-wielding assailants angered by the band's assaults on British tradition. That same year the group found itself essentially grounded when they could find no U.K. venues that would risk booking the Sex Pistols.

In January of 1978, the Sex Pistols took their act to America. They were accustomed to being the center of attention back home, and they were dismayed when their first audience comprised about five hundred ticket holders. The group then went on a tour with dates in the Deep South and Texas—not exactly fertile ground for British iconoclastic punks in the late seventies. They were greeted with hostility, confusion, and large doses of indifference. Along the way Sid's bouts of addiction and withdrawal were becoming too much to bear; at times he was too strung out to play onstage, and his vandalism and self-mutilation had lost any edge of humor or playfulness. Sid was turning into a parody of himself, and later that month Rotten left the band. Sid would suffer two overdoses the same January.

By mid year Sid was living in New York, burdened by his drug addiction and by similarly addicted girlfriend Nancy Spungen. He recorded a scathing cover of the standard "My Way," and performed gigs at Max's Kansas City and CBGB's. In October Sid was off the rails for good when he called police to the Chelsea Hotel room he shared with Spungen; officers found Spungen lying under the bathroom sink, stabbed to death. Vicious was arrested, charged with murder, and sent to notorious Riker's Island. He reportedly attempted suicide twice while he was there, despondent over the loss of Spungen. McLaren posted Vicious's bail, but the next February Sid took a fatal overdose of heroin apparently supplied to him by his mother. He died on Groundhog Day, 1979.

An Undignified End

Music fans winced collectively in 1979 upon hearing news that Sid Vicious's cremated remains had been dropped at London's Heathrow Airport and scattered on the floor.

Tainted Memories

"I still think of Sid. The whole thing was awful for him. There's no point. He died, and that's the end of it. I wish he was around, but only the way he was originally. All that self-destruction was just too much. You watch someone deteriorate before your eyes in the space of a year, and that's it. They erase any good memories you have of them."

—Johnny Rotten, from his autobiography Rotten: No Irish, No Blacks, No Dogs

Gene Vincent

"Race with the Devil"

The rock 'n' roll lifestyle was not without its travails for the former Eugene Vincent Craddock. Amid years of successful touring and hit records he also endured four marriages and divorces, near death in a car crash, a bum leg that doctors would suggest cutting off, and an eventual downward career spiral that would coincide with his own drinking and dark moods.

Vincent was released by the navy following a 1955 motorcycle accident that left him with a serious leg injury that would never properly heal. During one of his hospital stays he paid a fellow patient twenty-five dollars for a song called "Be-Bop-A-Lula." He recorded that tune, along with two others, and, in 1956, won an "Elvis Presley Soundalike Sweepstakes" that landed him a contract with Capitol Records. "Be-Bop-A-Lula" would hit the Top 10 that year (and eventually sell nine million copies by the time of Vincent's death). Vincent's image was tougher and harder-bitten than Elvis's, which audiences would discover in the 1956 film *The Girl Can't Help It*.

An essential component of Vincent's tough-guy image was his trademark limp, but it came with a cost—in 1957 he was fitted with a metal leg brace that he would be forced to wear for the rest of his life. Vincent and his band, the Blue Caps, remained near the top of the rock class in the waning years of the fifties, charting Top 20 with "Lotta Lovin'" in 1957 and maintaining a hearty touring schedule. When his fortunes sagged a bit, Vincent went overseas, where American rockers were greeted by adoring audiences. He had just finished a tour with fellow rock pioneer Eddie Cochran in 1960 when their hired taxi crashed on the way to London. Cochran was killed, and Vincent suffered serious injuries. Recovery was difficult for Vincent, and after his physical injuries healed he was tormented by the death of his friend. Heavy drinking and depression followed, along with a career decline.

Vincent spent much of the sixties touring—he was still a vital onstage presence, although his recorded efforts no longer saw much chart action. In 1969 Vincent played the Toronto Rock 'n' Roll Festival, along with the Doors, John Lennon, Chuck Berry, and Jerry Lee Lewis. The next year he veered in a country-rock direction, releasing the LP *I'm Back and I'm Proud*; though the release was lauded by critics, Vincent had long since lost the attention of the record-buying audience.

Meanwhile, Vincent's personal problems dogged him at every turn. He endured the dissolution of his fourth marriage, his drinking and depression plumbed new depths, and he continued to suffer chronic pain from his bad leg (in 1966, doctors had gone so far as to recommend amputation to treat it once and for all). It was clear that he was on the downward side of his rock 'n' roll career when, on September 12, 1971, he fell in his parents' house and ruptured a stomach ulcer. He was dead that same day of internal bleeding. Gene Vincent had started out as an Elvis-sound-alike contest winner with promising talent, but he was unable to sustain lasting rock success much beyond the fifties. His rocker image had always evoked trouble and turmoil, qualities that were in no small supply in Vincent's life.

ROCK AND ROLL HALL OF FAME
Inducted 1998

ESSENTIAL LISTENING
The Screaming End: The Best of Gene Vincent

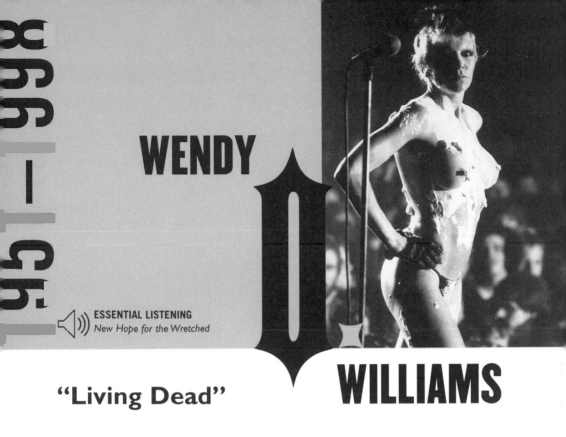

WENDY O. WILLIAMS

🔊)) **ESSENTIAL LISTENING**
New Hope for the Wretched

"Living Dead"

Plasmatics concert in the early eighties was a grab bag of fun including, but not limited to, the sight of guitars being sawed in half, cars blown up, and televisions smashed with a sledgehammer. The music was by and large unbearable noise, but audiences were in attendance to view the lady general of this art circus—Wendy O. Williams. Often dressed in little more than bondage pants and strategically placed shaving cream and electrical tape, Williams was a raging explosion of sex, hatred for authority, and anticonsumerism.

The Plasmatics were invented by Ron Swenson, a New York sex-show porno producer who saw Malcolm McLaren's success as the Sex Pistols's string puller and figured he'd do the same. He enlisted Williams, a former teenage runaway from upstate New York who'd been involved in Swenson's productions. The sandpaper-voiced Williams fronted a band of misfits who produced a loud, grating, punk-metal sound that was fairly awful on record. LPs *New Hope for the Wretched* and *Beyond the Valley of 1984* were grating curiosities that by and large gathered dust on record store shelves.

Live, the Plasmatics gathered a cult following eager to view Williams's latest outrage. She simulated masturbation with her microphone stand, wielded a variety of weapons of destruction, and strutted in a state of seminudity. Inevitably authorities were called in to protect paying crowds from the sight of a woman's breasts, and in 1981 Williams was arrested for public obscenity in Milwaukee and Cleveland. Williams didn't interact well with law enforcement, and she was beaten and hospitalized in Milwaukee after resisting arrest.

Throughout the rest of the eighties Williams toured and recorded alternately as a solo artist and with new Plasmatics lineups. She appeared in the film *Reform School Girls* in 1986 and popped up in an episode of TV's *McGyver*. By the early nineties she had vanished from the public eye and was reportedly deep into physical fitness and health food. A soul that had gravitated to such turmoil was undoubtedly a troubled one, however, and in 1998 a statement informed the public that Wendy O. Williams had committed suicide at age forty-eight. Her years of menace and mayhem were over.

Jackie Wilson
"Am I the Man?"

 ROCK AND ROLL HALL OF FAME
Inducted 1987

ESSENTIAL LISTENING
The Jackie Wilson Story

The Downside of Being a Ladies' Man
In 1961 Jackie Wilson was attacked by a female fan named Juanita Jones, who invaded his home in a fit of crazed idol worship. Jones pulled a gun and threatened to shoot herself; when Wilson tried to intervene, the gun went off and wounded Wilson in the stomach. He spent two weeks in the hospital recuperating, eventually being discharged with the bullet still inside him. Apparently the bullet was in a harmless but hard-to-access location, and it would remain with Wilson for the rest of his days.

Soul singer Jackie Wilson hasn't been remembered with as much reverence as James Brown or Sam Cooke—the two contemporaries with whom he is most often compared—but in his sixties heyday he was one of the most dynamic and captivating performers in America. His career had fallen on lean times by the mid-seventies, however, when he collapsed onstage and suffered a debilitating episode from which he would never recover. The details of his death are among the most tragic in pop music history, but the legacy of his recorded work rarely fails to elicit reactions ranging from tapping toes to downright elation.

Wilson came out of a rough part of Detroit and knew how to hold his own with anyone—he won a Golden Gloves boxing title while still in high school, competing under a false name. He envisioned a boxing career in his future but wisely took heed when his mother suggested developing his singing chops instead. Wilson had a great natural voice, rich and emotive, and in 1953 he was invited to replace his idol Clyde McPhatter in the doo-wop group Billy Ward and His Dominoes. He sang lead on a Top 20 hit for the group in 1956, then left to test the waters of a solo career.

Though he initially had a hard time stepping out of the Dominoes's shadow, Wilson soon established himself as one of the premiere R&B singers of the late fifties and early sixties. He would eventually chart more than a dozen hits on the charts, including " 'Reet Petite," "Lonely Teardrops," "Baby Workout," and "(Your Love Keeps Lifting Me) Higher and Higher." He was an athletic and sensual performer onstage, and was capable of working the female segment of his audience into a state of mass hysterical arousal. For a time, greatness was his.

Wilson's final chart single was in 1972; three years later saw him treading the boards of the oldies circuit. It was at such a show—Dick Clark's "Good Ol' Rock 'n' Roll" revue at the Latin Casino in Cherry Hill, New Jersey—where Wilson collapsed on September 29, 1975. He was in the middle of performing his signature song, "Lonely Teardrops," when he suffered a heart attack. Wilson struck his head falling, and fell into a coma that would last for four months. When he emerged, it was discovered that he had suffered substantial brain damage from oxygen deprivation. Jackie Wilson remained hospitalized, immobile and incapable of speech, until his death in 1984.

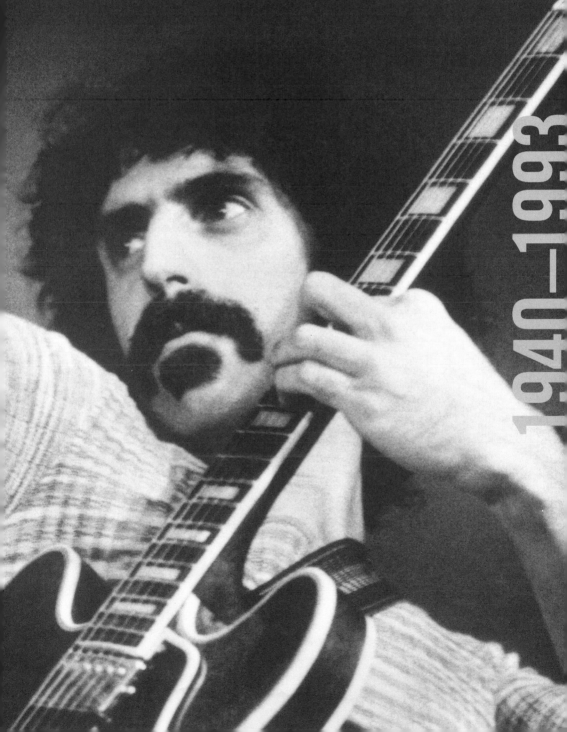

Frank Zappa

1940–1993

"Does Humor Belong in Music?"

H
e would never, ever be accused of conformity. Every fiber of Frank Zappa's being pushed hard in the direction of the subversive, the transgressive, and the outrageous. He was also an innovative guitarist, an ambitious bandleader, and an orchestral composer. Along the way he picked up an incisive social consciousness that led him to the halls of congress and the music world's version of the Scopes Monkey Trial—the PMRC hearings. An original who rarely evoked lukewarm reaction—it would have been anathema to his ethic—Zappa's totally original music career spanned parts of four decades and was stilled only by his death from cancer at fifty-two.

Zappa grew up in California steeped in fifties rock, R&B, and doo-wop, while also indulging in a taste for avant-garde classical composers at an early age. He learned guitar and studied music theory for a short time, then bounced around and eventually built a home studio in Cucamonga. After a short jail stay for producing "pornography" (he'd supplied an undercover cop with a tape of phony grunts and moans), Zappa joined a soul band that he christened the Mothers. They played the mid-sixties hippie scene in L.A., then secured a record deal. Already the band had a reputation for outrage and subversive social commentary, and for their first release they were compelled by their record company to rename themselves the Mothers of Invention.

Freak Out! was released in 1966, and lived up to its title; it was a southern Californian satirist's answer to flower-power psychedelia,

and instituted Zappa's vision of scatology, biting lampoons of social norms, and ambitiously experimental music. It was also a commercial dud, as was the following year's *Absolutely Free.* This time, though, Zappa expanded his palate even farther, adding chaotic sound jumbles and found-sound edits to increasingly accomplished playing. Zappa and the Mothers were prolific, going on to record *Lumpy Gravy, We're Only in It for the Money,* and *Uncle Meat,* to name a few titles from an increasingly hard-to-track catalogue.

In 1969 Zappa released a solo LP, *Hot Rats,* which was an ambitious mix of rock and jazz that prominently featured Zappa's guitar playing. Somehow he had managed to develop a guitar style that matched his vocals and lyrics—in his hands, the instrument would wander, then focus, sounding dirty and mad, then would abruptly snap into a run of concise notes most players would die to come up with. Zappa flitted from style to style, often producing tracks that straddled the divide between appreciation and mockery. Detractors would accuse Zappa of being a dilettante and a cut-and-paste hack; Zappa himself loved to argue, and would cut down all takers with his quick wit and acid tongue.

Throughout his long career Zappa also composed orchestral music and nursed an ambition to lead an orchestra. As early as 1967 he recorded the Mothers' *Lumpy Gravy* with orchestral accompaniment, and in 1970 he performed his *200 Motels* film score with the L.A. Philharmonic. Zappa was insanely prolific, veering from one interest to the next and releasing more than sixty LPs by the time of his death. His greatest commercial success came in

1974 with *Apostrophe (')*, which contained fairly
accessible jazz-pop and simplified narratives
such as "Don't Eat the Yellow Snow." For the
most part, though, Zappa would produce scores
of albums for a cult audience, most of them
produced in his home studio. His ever-shifting
band would also back him on a long succession
of international tours.

To the general public, Zappa was a strange
figure who emerged from time to time with a
novelty single that usually incorporated his
mocking, knowing voice over a percolating
hyperprecise backing track. First in this vein was
1979's "Dancin' Fool," a Top 50 hit lampooning
(or maybe celebrating, who knew) disco. Even
more successful was 1982's "Valley Girl," which
featured daughter Moon Unit speaking
Encino-ese. All the while Zappa released live
recordings and intricate studio LPs, impeccably
performed and often so tasteless as to inspire
hoots of nervous laughter.

In 1985 Zappa went to Congress and spoke
to a Senate subcommittee investigating obscenity
in popular music. Zappa caustically criticized
the panel (including a memorably patronizing Al
Gore) for hypocrisy and promoting censorship.
It was a hall-of-fame performance, and Zappa
came off as the most intelligent and creative
person in the room (perhaps no great feat, but
still . . .). The Senate hearings seemed to crystal-
lize Zappa's vision of artistic freedom and personal expression, concepts he would champion
for the rest of his life—notably in his hilarious
1989 autobiography *The Real Frank Zappa Book*.

In 1991 the world learned that Zappa was
suffering from prostate cancer. He never took
drugs or drank—although he was a prodigious
smoker and consumed rivers of coffee—and
would have seemed an unlikely candidate for an
early exit. Zappa continued to work at the same
rate. In 1993 he released a new classical work,
The Yellow Shark, that surprised many with its
high quality and innovative arrangements. A flurry
of new releases stopped only after Zappa's
death on December 4, 1993. He died at home,
quietly, with his family.

With his death, the world lost one of the
most original voices in rock 'n' roll. Fans can be
comforted by the dizzying variety of material
Zappa produced in his long career, spanning
rock, classical, jazz, and the mutant hybrid of all
of the above and more that was his bailiwick.
Perhaps most important, Zappa refused to
distinguish between high and low art, mixing
classical strings with pee-pee-ca-ca humor
without batting an eye—or expecting us to.

ROCK AND ROLL HALL OF FAME
Inducted 1995

ESSENTIAL LISTENING
Hot Rats
Joe's Garage Acts I, II & III
The Yellow Shark